Chasing ideas

To Lucinda, Spencer, Alexander, and Tommaso
and children everywhere:
The world is yours – may you be positive, observant,
creative, self-reliant, and happy.

Chasing ideas

The fun of freeing your child's imagination

Christine Durham

Jessica Kingsley Publishers
London and Philadelphia

...ralia and New Zealand by Finch Publishing Pty Limited,
... 120, Lane Cove, NSW, 1595, Australia. ISBN 1 876451 18 1.

... by Jessica Kingsley Publishers in 2006

Philadelphia, PA 19106, USA

www.jkp.com

Text designed and typeset in Adobe Garamound by Dizign
Illustrations by Chris Morgan

Library of Congress Cataloging in Publication Data
    Durham, Christine, 1944-
      Chasing ideas : the fun of freeing your child's imagination / Christine Durham. -- Rev. ed.
        p. cm.
      Includes bibliographical references and index.
      ISBN-13: 978-1-84310-460-5 (pbk. : alk. paper)
      ISBN-10: 1-84310-460-1 (pbk. : alk. paper) 1. Imagination in children. 2. Cognition in children. 3.
Child rearing. I. Title.
      BF723.I5D87 2006
      649'.51--dc22

                    2006011861

British Library Cataloguing in Publication Data
A CIP catalogue record for this book is available from the British Library

ISBN-13: 978 1 84310 460 5
ISBN-10: 1 84310 460 1

Printed and bound in Great Britain by
Athenaeum Press, Gateshead, Tyne and Wear

Contents

Introduction: Falling in love with ideas

Love is looking outward together in the same direction.

Antoine De Saint Exupéry 1900–1944

Chasing ideas with children is a highlight of my life. To be with children who are busting with ideas, eyes shining, cheeks pink with excitement – the fun and fervour of the chase, being carried along with ideas, brains on fire – is unbelievably thrilling and satisfying. Being the mother of four, I've had such wonderful fun chasing and playing with ideas with my kids. For over a decade as a classroom teacher, and a further ten years running over 4000 thinking workshops with young students, I have found that chasing ideas has connected children with ideas in an exciting, powerful way.

Nothing is more important than helping your children to think for themselves. Nothing is likely to be more effective, rewarding and encouraging than practical hand-in-hand discovery and thinking together. Chasing ideas empowers your children, makes them better, brighter thinkers – it whets their curiosity, their powers of observation and their awareness so that they concentrate, listen, think for themselves and express their ideas clearly. This in turn helps them understand issues, solve problems and make thoughtful decisions.

In this book you will find ideas to help you to move your comfort zone so that you can confidently open up discussions about important concepts and questions in an adventurous and playful way. These concepts will include truth, justice, trust, power, good and bad, and ownership. Chasing and playing with ideas about things that don't matter at the time, but will really matter sometime, puts in place a foundation of thoughts about all sorts of issues, to revisit and build on.

By chasing ideas, children find and clarify their own values in an atmosphere of exploration and discovery. They will gain understanding and knowledge about the adults in their life; they will gain experience and confidence in expressing their opinions, and they will start to see the complexities in many issues. They will also develop a greater appreciation of the process of communication and community.

By using everyday events (it could be eating baked beans, buying bread, or having a hair cut), and everyday objects (the moon, a lemon, a sponge, a teddy bear biscuit) and stories (anecdotes, books, films and television programs), you can open up and build discussions with children. They will think about themselves, the world and their place in it. This will grow and develop their self-awareness, self-acceptance and self-esteem. Together you will construct a foundation of ideas to revisit and build upon in the days and years to follow. You will empower your children and enrich your relationship.

These thinking aloud discussions can take place anywhere, anytime: in the car, having dinner, washing up or when you are taking the dog for a walk. With a wide variety of ideas, information and thinking tools, you can grow discussions with children. They will not only gain knowledge, but they will also learn to use this knowledge to compare, to find connections in issues and to be able to judge. Playing with ideas is important because 'thinking well' is a skill that will stay with your children for the rest of their lives.

In chasing ideas with children we need to be managers, leaders and friends. As managers we have authority and take charge, we think logically and instruct and work to promote self-esteem. As leaders we inspire and influence our children. We build on their strengths, sense opportunities, set examples and search for their potential. As friends we share time, thoughts and laughter.

> You sort out your ideas when you talk.

Children can also be managers, leaders and friends to us. Sometimes they will take charge of discussions, they will influence and create opportunities, and they will share ideas and humour with us.

We can encourage our children to focus on how they go about thinking (so that they don't just concentrate on giving the 'right' answer). We can explore how we think, learn and communicate. We can demonstrate how to tackle puzzles and problems. We can provide important thinking moments by creating opportunities for significant experiences to happen, and we can witness the magic moments when children connect with an idea that fascinates them and whets their curiosity to explore more and more ideas.

From childhood I've had a passion for thinking and a fascination and curiosity about ideas. My father always regarded me as having interesting, thoughtful comments to share with him. We would go for 'talking walks', a sort of game where he would treat me as an intellectual equal and ask my opinion about many things. It was so great to be treated as an adult, and to have my opinions listened to in a way that made me feel that everything I said was interesting, even if my ideas needed modification or revisiting. By being curious and talking about things that didn't matter, or didn't appear to be significant at the time, but came to matter later, many 'files' were opened in my head so that I could refer to and build on what we discussed.

> Discussions
> strengthen
> relationships.

I learnt a lot. I learnt to challenge myself and I learnt to express my thoughts. I had lots of practice arguing the toss with my father, who often played devil's advocate. Dad's ability to listen to and believe in me has helped me to think about and to cope with all sorts of difficulties. My parents obviously had a vision of the sort of person they wanted me to be, and they put time and effort into providing opportunities for growth and development in an engaging, entertaining and challenging way. Our discussions also strengthened our relationship.

As a teacher, I am constantly entranced and excited by the thoughtful, flexible, open and creative way children rise to thinking challenges. Children thrive on being asked their opinion about 'big' issues, issues that as adults we would not generally think to discuss with them.

This book has been in the pipeline for over a decade. My office at home was crammed with folders and notes, and thousands of words had gathered on my computer. Countless hours have been spent thinking and discussing topics and ideas with everyone: my family, my students and my agents, Jacinta and Jenny. Then something happened that brought all my thoughts together – I became a grandmother for the first time.

On my daily hospital visits to my dear daughter and my darling granddaughter, I'd pass the street light pole that nearly took my life in a ghastly car accident a decade ago. I was so thankful that I was still here to experience the joys of grandmother-hood; I was acutely aware that you can be here one moment and gone the next.

Chasing Ideas shares my experiences and discoveries about getting children to think. This book is a gift of ideas, to allow parents new and old, grandparents, and friends and teachers, to help children to develop curiosity, attentiveness, knowledge and alertness so that they are not caught unawares, so that they do not sleep their life away and miss so much that can be absorbing and enlightening and enriching.

When I hold my granddaughter Lucinda I wish I could be a fairy godmother. I want to wave a magic wand and give her a life full of health and happiness and wisdom. I want her to have the gift of thinking that will help her to be happy. I want Lucinda to be positive and optimistic about life. I want her to have the gift of thinking that will help her to be wise; to have common sense in an uncommon degree, as Samuel Taylor Coleridge put it. I want her to be curious, observant, attentive, perceptive, self-reliant, confident and independent. I want her to be empowered so that she can get cracking and get stuck into things. These qualities come from the way we think. *Chasing Ideas* will help her.

Chasing Ideas will help children:

* To be empowered and to have confidence.
* To learn to sort and prioritise information; this will help them to develop thoughtful decision-making strategies, so they can make informed decisions throughout their lives.
* To have curiosity to find out about things. They will know that complicated problems can be broken into smaller parts, and that these parts can be investigated step by step.
* To be sensitive to the atmosphere and to listen to what others are saying. This will help them understand where people are coming from and where they are going.

* To find what they consider are priorities. This will help them to know what to fight for, and make commitments to, and what to compromise on.
* To understand that ideas are complicated, and that everyone makes mistakes sometime. This will help them to admit their mistakes, to learn from them, and to forgive themselves and others.

Chasing Ideas will help you:

* Make a difference in the lives of your children by helping them to think in an enhanced way.
* Build understanding and trust in your relationship with your children.
* Understand the benefits and value of good thinking.
* Give you practice in chasing ideas, so that good thinking becomes a habit in your family.
* Acquire thinking tools to open up issues important in the life of your children.
* Encourage a positive outlook embracing self-acceptance and self-esteem.
* Find and grasp opportunities for chasing ideas with your children.
* Give you practice telling stories to your children, and listening to your children's stories to help explain and understand different points of view.
* Make thinking a hobby that can be carried out anywhere and anytime, so your children will always have their own thoughts for company.

Chasing ideas with children

All children paint like geniuses.
What we do to them so quickly dulls the ability.
Pablo Picasso 1881–1973

When I was a child I was enthralled by the romance and beauty of the mighty ship, the *Titanic*, the epitome of sophistication, design and technology being sunk in those silent, inky black, icy waters. The figurehead of civilisation, scuttled and sunk by a simple lump of ice. The might of nature, victorious over the brilliance and complexity of humans. This concept and the mystery of the story of the *Titanic* still capture the imagination of children; they are fascinated by it.

On board the *Titanic*

Recently, the *Titanic* floated to the surface of a discussion I was having with a group of eight-year-olds. We were discussing a charming Mexican story that concerned the idea about 'rich' people and 'poor' people. After the fourth child began talking by referring to the *Titanic*, I was nonplussed. What on earth did the *Titanic* have to do with this Mexican story? My head was buzzing with all sorts of queries: Don't these kids know what we're talking about? And Hello-o! Have I missed something? Then the penny dropped. The movie *Titanic* (which they'd all seen and were passionate about) was a clear example of the class system and the comparison between rich and poor people. 'You little beauties!' I whispered under my breath. Without fail, kids come up trumps thinking about connecting and clarifying ideas.

We had an excited, animated discussion (and a huge argument) about the good and bad points of being rich or poor. When we looked for curious points, some wonderful sweeping statements were born from the children's ideas. Notions of 'goodness' or 'badness' and whether a person is good or bad depending on whether they are rich or poor were discussed, and generalisations were examined with great fervour. Convincing reasons and examples were argued about and 'proof' was debated.

Who or what sank the *Titanic*?

I wondered this question aloud (as if the children had made me think of it). For some, the question was like a red rag to a bull (just as I'd hoped). They were leaping about on their seats because they knew the answer. 'It was an iceberg!' (Don't you know anything?) No sooner were the words out of their mouths than I could see realisation dawning. Oh, it wasn't that simple.

Some of the things they identified as playing a part in the *Titanic* sinking included the iceberg, the owners wanting to make lots of money trying to break the record from London to New York, speed, and thinking the ship was unsinkable. The more we discussed things the more it became apparent that an idea (the *Titanic* is unsinkable) was responsible for sinking the great ship. Powerful stuff!

Responsibility and blame

Was the person who thought of describing the ship 'unsinkable' responsible? Was it the owners, the builders, the designers, the press, the promoters? Maybe because people thought the *Titanic* could not sink they did not take as much care as they should have. Did the men on watch fail to recognise danger because of ignorance about icebergs or because of carelessness? There were design faults. Was this because of ignorance, priorities (money being spent on luxuries not safety), not being built strongly enough, not having enough propellers to stop in a hurry, or was it due to a lack of knowledge about technology?

If you were one of the construction workers and you saw something you did not consider correct or strong enough, should you report it to the bosses or just do your job? If you ignore taking responsibility for a safety issue are you partly to blame if something goes wrong? The captain came under fire for making the wrong judgements. Responsibility, priorities and blame were teased out and discussed, with current examples used to compare and contrast ideas. Lack of experience, people not being alert because they thought it was unsinkable, irresponsibility, ignorance, trust and belief all played a part in the tragedy.

It's interesting to play the 'If only' game by trying to find as many things as possible that might have saved the day and saved the ship: 'If only the iceberg were smaller'; 'If only they had paid attention to the warnings'.

Discussing the *Titanic* in this way helped the children to think, understand and make connections. When you're chasing ideas, don't just direct your children to the points that you think are important – rather, let them lead with the issues *they* find interesting. These sorts of discussions are neverending because you can use points raised to make connections to other issues. Don't forget to use your discussions to find comparisons and similarities with everyday happenings and news events. It's so exciting to extend and unfold your discussion and to be able to find other examples of responsibility and blame, experience and priorities. Discuss and argue about new ideas using your original ideas as yardsticks.

Why did so many people die?

If you discuss the *Titanic* with your children (especially if they have seen the movie), the question 'Why did so many people die?' will come up. This is a great example of something that does not answer the question we have been examining (Who or what sank the *Titanic*?) but poses another question altogether. 'Why did so many people die?' Because there weren't enough lifeboats. 'Why weren't there enough lifeboats?' Because they needed the deck space for walking, because lifeboats looked messy, and because people thought they did not need them if the *Titanic* was unsinkable.

Why did the first lifeboats go off nearly empty?

Answering
questions requires
empathy.

To answer this question we need to empathise and put ourselves in the place of those people on this magnificent unsinkable ship, looking down at the freezing water thinking, I'm safer here than in one of those little boats! Then it was too late. They should have been prepared. They should have had a safety drill. They needed leadership not panic.

Instances of panic and flight and death, perhaps at a football match or a fire, can be discussed to understand more about how the people must have felt sinking in the middle of an icy ocean so long ago.

Should the *Titanic* be raised?

Another interesting discussion you can have about the *Titanic* is wondering, should the *Titanic* be raised? Reasons to raise the *Titanic* could include showing what things were like in the past; enabling people to see the incredible ship; making lots of money from tourists; giving the dead funerals; selling the jewels on board and using the money to create a lasting memory of the story.

If the *Titanic* is raised some of the problems might include: Where would the ship be put? Would it show lack of respect for the dead if the victims' bones were disturbed? It would be terribly expensive as the *Titanic* would be very difficult to raise, resting deep in the ocean and broken into pieces as it is. Perhaps it is now home to fish, and we should not disturb their habitat.

There are a lot of curious points about raising the *Titanic*. For example, who owns the *Titanic*? Are finders keepers? Would the raised *Titanic* be one of the greatest tourist attractions in the world? What makes something a good tourist attraction? What sort of things do tourists like to see? Why?

Our discussion continued to gain momentum and depth. When I asked the next question, I said it would be the hardest question the children would ever have to answer at school. I carried on a little about how university students and grown-ups would find it unbelievably difficult to answer. Children love this sort of thing, and by now they were busting with pride and curiosity.

Who should be saved?

Children love a challenge, and here it was: 'If you had to choose, who would go into the limited number of lifeboats?' They had to give reasons for their choice.

The children loved 'playing God'. They discussed the young and the old, the important, the rich, the poor, the nice and kind, the selfish, women, men and children, the good and the bad. To put people in pigeonholes like this we found we needed to come up with definitions. What does young mean? What does old mean?

We had some wonderful discussions about 'old'. One student defined it as 'someone with grey hair', another as 'over fifty'. This led to discussions about perception being in the head of the person – like beauty in the eye of the beholder (to quote a student). Young and old have so much to do with comparisons and the age you are yourself. If old were defined as sixty, if you were sixty-one would you have to die if old people were not allowed in the lifeboats? Some children thought that drowning in icy water would be so horrible that the old deserved to live.

If there were bad people aboard (How would you know if someone is bad? How do you define bad? Murderers?), should they be left to go down with the ship? Some children argued that bad people and murderers should be saved so that they had a chance to repent and change. This led us to chase ideas in another direction. What is the difference between murder and manslaughter? What if you didn't mean to kill the person but it was just a result of an accident for instance? If you were sorry for what you had done does that mean it is no longer bad? It was time for big confessions here! Children confessed to losing their temper or doing things that were out of character … were these things counted in judging them as 'bad'?

Back to the *Titanic*. What about children and babies? They hadn't had time to live much yet, so did that mean they had the right to live more than older people? But a boat full of babies and children would be especially vulnerable in the dark and cold. If mothers and their babies and children were to be saved, that would not be fair to the children without mothers or the women without babies. Would it be safer to have some men to help look after the women and children? How could you choose? If you said all good and kind people could be saved, how would you prove that the people were good and kind?

One child gave the example that if a person said, 'No, you go first, I don't deserve to be saved' they might be kind, therefore they should be saved. Or they might be smart and just pretending to be kind.

Putting people in the lifeboat because they were the ones that were likely to survive was another possible issue.

The notion of some people needing to be 'chosen' was of great concern to the children. It is an issue that in the future they may have to face … whether in international law or choosing the recipient for a heart transplant. What about the class system? If you pay more do you have the right to get saved first? (If you have the money to pay for a heart transplant should you have first choice?)

I'm sure you can see that when these eight-year-olds were discussing the *Titanic* they were playing with ideas. They were sorting out their ideas. They were thinking about believing and proof, relationships and values, trust and rights, responsibility and ownership, justice and fairness, blame, truth and lies. They were judging 'good' and 'bad', finding the difference between deliberate and accidental and exploring notions of perception, problems and mysteries.

They were asking and answering questions, using similes, metaphors, analogies and stories to justify their points. They were

playing devil's advocate with each other. They were examining priorities and judging their own ideas and the ideas of others: exploring ideas in a playful way.

A discussion like this with children is wonderful and exhausting! For a start you have to really listen carefully and concentrate. You need to be ready to play devil's advocate. Say something obviously 'way out' to get them to argue their point, enthuse about their ideas, ask them to 'tell me more', be ready to interpret or make an analogy such as, 'Do you mean like …?' and be ready to throw some new ideas into the arena. Get excited, be amazed, suddenly understand a point, make your own interpretation, or link the idea to something similar and relevant.

Chasing ideas lets children explore ideas in a supporting, reassuring atmosphere. What better way to grow their confidence, vocabulary and understanding.

Thinking aloud can bind and create a strong family

'Strong families bend in the wind – they have the ability to adapt to changing circumstances and stressful situations, and see crises as opportunities to grow. They're also bonded together not just by love, but by a kind of glue created over time by a mixture of things like respect for individuality, shared experiences and shared beliefs.'

Thinking aloud can reinforce strong parent/ child relationships and empower the child

'I knew I could do anything, go anywhere, do anything I wanted to do because Mum and Dad told me I could. I remember times when Dad said, 'Let's you and me go for a drive,' and, for a short while, I was the centre of his world and he listened to what was going on in my life …'

Chasing ideas can provide parents with ideas for worthwhile thinking time with their children. 'Too little time,' says Barbara Holborrow, retired Children's Court magistrate, 'erodes two of those qualities which build family strength – good communication and spending time together … There's not enough time to explore ideas with our kids, to just sit around and chew the fat. Sometimes the most important communication is done when you least expect it.'

The ten basic principles

A friend is one before whom I may think aloud.
Ralph Waldo Emerson 1803–1882

There are ten basic principles for chasing ideas with children. You will probably find you already have and use similar ideas in a general sense. Keep in mind and use these vital points to help you focus on the way your children think and communicate as your friends and thinking partners as you chase ideas.

The principles for chasing ideas are:

1. Show your children that you love them and their ideas
2. Build their self-respect, self-esteem and self-confidence
3. Expect great ideas
4. Be perceptive and aware
5. Let your children copy what you model
6. Make children aware of the magic and nuance of words
7. Make it fun and play with ideas
8. Listen actively
9. Ask open questions
10. Stories are important

1. Show your children that you love them and their ideas

In chasing ideas with children, love is all-important. Show your interest, appreciation and love for them; show them you enjoy their company. Have fun with them, share their secrets and their pain, and use every opportunity to strengthen your relationships. Playing with ideas, exploring notions and chasing ideas with children is an obvious demonstration of love. Love for the children and love of ideas. Create and provide opportunities, set the mood and atmosphere so that children will fall in love with ideas.

We need patience to wait and listen to the whole question or idea rather than jumping in with the answer before the whole question is asked. This is a trap I sometimes fall into. In my enthusiasm to demonstrate I am understanding and following what is being said, I answer questions before they are asked and I sometime finish sentences. Children are constantly being inundated with conflicting messages, so we need to give them thinking time; time for reflection so that they can work out what they *really* think.

> Children need time to think.

Adults and children are partners, collaborators and team members in the thinking game. Let your children see your admiration, your belief that they have great ideas. Fill your chasing ideas time with laughter and love. Aim for your children to experience what I call the Thinkers' High, when they feel high as a kite, charmed and fascinated, satisfied by and full of wonder at their own ideas, and their heads full of thinking.

We want our children to have confidence in themselves, to believe that they are valuable members of society, to take responsibility for themselves and their actions. We want them to have open, enquiring minds.

The dictionary defines encouragement as the giving of courage: to make bold, to put heart into, to urge, to promote courage. We can encourage our children to think. There is nothing more encouraging than genuine interest and praise for achievement. Our children will come up with better ideas if they know their ideas are appreciated. Say to them several times a day: 'What an idea!', 'Well done!', or 'Fantastic!' Creativity grows with praise.

Encouragement is crucial to make the tentative shoots of an idea blossom. Encourage children to think critically and creatively by carefully listening to what they say. Give them time and your undivided attention, in words and body language. Convey the message: 'You are an interesting person; your thoughts and ideas are thought provoking'. Make an opportunity to discuss everyday happenings, events, ideas and concepts with them.

Set out together to discover the world. Be detectives, ask questions, search for the truth. Listen, think and comment a day or so after your child has made an interesting point: 'I've been thinking about what you said. It makes a lot of sense to me and has helped me understand that ...' and give an example that fits into the concepts you have been discussing.

It's our ideas that make us who we are. This thought hit me when I eventually 'came to' in Intensive Care, after the car accident, unable to move or speak. My mind was imprisoned inside my uncooperative body. My mind and what I thought was 'me'. My ideas were all I owned. My ideas, my belief in myself, and a huge amount of effort have led me to where I am today and where I will go in the future. When you think about it, for most of us our face isn't our fortune. Our *own ideas* are our fortune. It is how we handle the cards life deals us, or how we manage to get the 'right' cards, that determines not only our present and future situations but also our happiness.

We can encourage our children to think courageously, hopefully, optimistically and resourcefully, to look for possibilities and opportunities, and to use their initiative to turn 'bad' things into something positive. To quote my daughter Helen: 'Mum, you're always trying to turn a piece of poo into a rose!'

Empathy, understanding and compassion are important if we are going to find the 'right' things to talk about. People only really listen to, or pay attention to things that interest or directly concern them. Adults need empathy and a certain degree of mental telepathy to fossick out the ideas that will really interest their children. You need to understand and translate ideas so that they will appeal to your children. Get on the same wavelength, and you will find yourself laughing, saying, 'You've stolen *my* idea!'

2. Build their self-respect, self-esteem and self-confidence

Raising self-esteem is a major goal of chasing ideas. When you chase ideas and play with them, encourage your children to have a positive belief in themselves. Promote their belief that, 'I can do it, I can think well, I can even teach and show my parents a thing or two!' We want our children to have self-respect, high self-esteem and self-confidence.

We need to encourage a Virtuous Circle (not a vicious circle) where self-confidence leads to motivation, motivation leads to better brighter thinking, and better brighter thinking leads to self-confidence.

The Virtuous Circle

I think I can → I can

Self-confidence   Self-confidence

Motivation ← Success

Compare the characteristics of children with low self-esteem with those of children with high self-esteem. Children with low self-esteem are not able to take responsibility for their actions, they don't take risks and they play it safe by avoiding risk-taking situations. They blame themselves or others for their own failure, they are suspicious and oversensitive, they need constant reassurance and material rewards. They have difficulty concentrating, they get frustrated easily, and they're easily influenced by others.

> Raise your child's self-esteem.

Children with high self-esteem trust their own ability. They are able to take risks and act independently, they are able to make choices and are able to accept challenges and responsibility. They have a good sense of humour, they are confident and resourceful and they are able to learn from their mistakes. Raising your child's self-esteem is a major goal of chasing ideas.

3. Expect great ideas

Like a self-fulfilling prophecy, how we are treated by others will affect how we see ourselves. Treat your children as interesting, thoughtful, intelligent people and they will reward you with interesting ideas.

In a study, teachers were given the 'wrong' achievement test results for some of their primary school students. The specialist teacher administering the test gave a higher score than was justified to some individual children. In a subsequent achievement test, at the end of that school year, the students given a higher score showed a great improvement in their test results. These students had been treated as if they were 'clever' and with the added faith in their ability they had responded very well. That is food for thought.

In a recent study undertaken in nursing homes, residents were cared for in a kinder, gentler atmosphere with classical music, a higher standard of meals with tablecloths and wine, and more attention from the staff. The residents exhibited greater wellbeing and calmness.

4. Be perceptive and aware

When I was a young girl, I once spied a bit of string dangling on a fence. Mum had been trying to find some string just that morning. She needed it to tie up a rosebush that our pet lamb Baa had started to munch on. Having string on my mind, I noticed the piece and proudly took it home for Mum. She was so pleased by this surprise gift that I came to the conclusion there was nothing Mum liked more than bits of string. As a consequence, I constantly had my eyes peeled to find bits of string, and soon we had a garden shed festooned with them.

It sounds obvious to state that we only see what we're looking for. If we are looking for interesting happenings and stories to share with our children we will see them. If we share and point out our interest in ideas and concepts, our children will keep an eye out for stories to share with us.

We need to pay attention, to read between the lines and notice all the interesting ideas put forward by our children. We must be vigilant and fossick for ideas in films, news reports or happenings that have relevance to our children's lives. Sometimes it will be necessary to find a way to make a certain idea fascinating to our children.

Timing is important. Through being perceptive and aware you can find just the right time to discuss a certain issue. Being ready and willing to embark on a chasing idea discussion when an issue naturally comes up is crucial. Some of the most valuable and meaningful discussions will happen when you least expect them.

Time is also important. Some ideas need time for reflection. With time, you and your children will come up with worthwhile opinions.

Awareness about communication is vital. Communication is so much more than words. Children are individual 'magic puddings'; moving composites of ideas and thoughts, preconceptions and prejudices, feelings and experiences. We need to take their attitudes and ideas into account when we are communicating with them. Where you're trying to grasp and follow your children's ideas, be aware of all the nonverbal messages and their body language.

5. Let children copy what you model

Ralph Waldo Emerson said that what you do speaks so loudly people can't hear what you say. Children are fantastic copiers. Every day in everything you do, you are providing a model for your children to copy. They watch how you behave. My 'copycat' granddaughter Lucinda (nearly two) recently got into my makeup, applying lipstick and even smacking her little lips together. She'd obviously observed and absorbed a great deal about the application of lipstick. Unfortunately, she had also observed her dad shaving, and she managed to shave her cheek. Ouch!

Children acquire values and beliefs just from observing you. They watch you to learn about self-discipline, tolerance, cooperation, respecting others, having manners, being aware of emotions, dealing with stress and disappointment, and being persistent.

Children will accept and copy your behaviour. If you demonstrate an open, questioning mind, it will seem normal for them to look at the world with a questioning, curious mind. There's an old saying that an open mind opens minds, and a closed mind closes minds. You need to engage in active listening, wondering and asking open-ended questions.

> Your actions speak so loudly that your children can't hear your words.

Present an optimistic view of the world. When you make a mistake or things go wrong, demonstrate how you can think about the issues, improve things or at least learn from your mistakes, so that in the future you have ideas to help you decide or choose.

6. Make children aware of the magic and nuance of words

Help your children to grow their vocabulary so they can accurately describe their thoughts. For a child, one word has ten meanings (for example the word 'say'), for an adult ten words have one meaning (for example instead of the word 'say' an adult might choose from: speak, utter, articulate, declare, pronounce, state, verbalise, answer, reply, exclaim). Share words with children, suggest alternative words, fine-tune the words and the meanings you are trying to convey. Make it a game and a challenge to find just the right word to express that thought. Describe the beach in the early morning, explain why you liked/didn't like that movie and tell a story about what happened at home or in the office today so that your children can understand and empathise. In turn, they can describe the park or what interesting ideas they have had.

Open up your children's insight so that together you can make discoveries, invent hypotheses, test and judge your concepts and apply them to what you've figured out in your own lives.

7. Make it fun and play with ideas

Humour and laughter play a key role in capturing and holding interest so make your children laugh to hold their attention. Play and joke with ideas in an entertaining way. Tease, tantalise and fascinate your children with ideas. Be captivated and astonished by their ideas.

Chase ideas, mess about with them, turn them this way and that. Play with your children's ideas – pay close attention to them, interpret them, paraphrase them. 'Is that what you mean?' 'Is it like …?' Be full of anticipation, listen and be prepared to change your thoughts on a topic if your children can provide a persuasive argument. Accept their views in a nonjudgemental way. Listen carefully, don't jump to conclusions or make snap judgements as it takes time, patience and humour to unravel ideas.

Have faith in your children's ideas and enjoy chasing ideas with them. Remember: 'The mind once stretched by a new idea never returns to its original dimension.' (Ralph Waldo Emerson)

8. Listen actively

When you listen actively you show respect and tolerance; you use eye contact, you nod and lean forward, and show with your body language that you're interested. By careful, thoughtful listening, by adding ideas or asking questions, you examine and develop a concept – you reach out and connect to the 'feel' of the idea, as well as the information.

Listening with understanding and empathy can be confronting, as it forces you to question your own beliefs, and look at issues from different angles and perspectives. However, listening, questioning and showing curiosity, are powerful ways to interest children in the grey areas between the black and white of issues.

Use the hypothetical to examine issues and listen to ideas in a different way – from another angle, in another context: 'If we do this … then …' Look at the issue from someone else's perspective. 'If she said that, she must be assuming …' Look for connections you can make with other ideas. Give your children opportunities to give reasons for their own views. Listen sensitively.

Actively listen to your discussions to pick up on important notions. Chasin ideas is not just chatting, it is discussing ideas with the purpose of understanding more about ideas that help make sense of the world.

The golden rules of active listening

* Do respect the other person's ideas
* Do nurture the discussion like a delicate plant
* Do water the discussion with encouragement
* Do feed the discussion with praise
* Do give the discussion lots and lots of positive strokes
* Don't be bossy and 'know it all'
* Don't interrupt
* Don't pull the discussion to bits
* Don't foist your ideas on your children

Adults and children must be active, not passive, when listening to each other experimenting with thoughts and ideas. Active listening allows children and adults to feel as if they are all winners since everyone's thoughts are visited and revisited in an interested, considerate way.

9. Ask open questions

Asking questions, answering questions and wondering about how to solve problems will help your children to think creatively and critically. Value different ways of solving problems and discuss the repercussions and consequences of different solutions.

Children need to learn about questions. Simple (or closed) questions require only simple thinking to answer them. The answer is 'simple' or 'closed' because there is only one correct answer. To answer a simple question you use your memory and the knowledge you have or can find. For example, to answer the question 'How many books are on the table?', you would count the books or, if you can't count or you can't see the table, you would ask someone to count them for you. To answer the question 'What is an elephant bird?', you would consult an encyclopedia, contact a museum or surf the Internet.

By comparison the question, 'Docs your mum dye her hair?' is also a simple question, but answering it might not be so simple. It depends on Mum's openness about people knowing 'the truth'. If she's dyed her hair purple or green the question is simple. The simple answer is, 'Yes.' But if Mum has 'touched up' her grey hair, and this is a secret not to be divulged under threat of death, the answer becomes complicated and open. There's no simple 'right' answer to this question. This question requires intricate, complicated, mental gymnastics to answer it so as to (a) not be in Mum's bad books and (b) retain some credibility with the questioner!

Open questions have many different answers, with perhaps no answer seeming to be 'the correct' answer. Frequently, open questions lead to more questions. For example, in the question about Mum dyeing her hair, the answer might depend on:

* A definition of what is dyed hair (a permanent colour or a wash-out colour, a marked change of hair colour or a subtle, almost unnoticeable colour change)
* The value your family puts on telling the truth (or accepting 'twisting' the truth and white lies)
* The intent of the person asking the question

Some open questions

What do you know?
What do you think?
What helped you decide that?
What helped you to make up your mind?
Do you have any more questions about it?
Can you adapt what we've been talking about to something else?
What do you find curious about that idea?
How do you feel now?
What does it remind you of?
Can you surprise me with a new idea about ...?

* How the information about Mum dyeing her hair will be used
* Your age. If you are the child being asked the question, your age and understanding will affect how you answer the question

Open questions open up the topic being discussed. This type of question is not asking for facts alone. To answer an open question you need to analyse, evaluate, interpret and make links and connections and judge. Open questions require complex thinking. Open questions grow discussions. Help your children to formulate open questions by discussing the topic further, patiently find out what they are attempting to understand. You could have a competition to find out who can ask the hardest questions about the topic.

10. Stories are important

Stories hold ideas, provide examples of ideas or lead to other ideas. Stories can form a link between children and adults.

Stories provide an interesting framework to hold ideas about important concepts. Stories lead the teller or listener to consider new ideas. Stories can be used as the vehicle to present and explore ideas. Stories contain an element of fun, entertainment, adventure, exploration and imagination. Stories can be built up, built on, changed, adapted and used in many ways to fit the age, experience and important happenings in the life of children. Stories can be told anywhere – in the car, walking, doing the dishes or waiting at the doctor's.

Recent studies in the world of business show that a chief characteristic of leaders is their ability to tell stories so that others can understand an idea or a vision. There is much anecdotal evidence to show that when a leader tells a story people understand and follow. For example Jack Welch, Chief Executive of General Electric, routinely tells stories about the 'grocery store' that is the global company. This analogy captures the interest and imagination of his audience and allows them to grasp the concepts.

Through chasing ideas, you and your children will become immersed in stories. You'll share and make up stories to make an analogy, explain a connection or similarity or difference, and to explain a point of view.

3

Thinking about thinking

All knowledge has its origins in our perceptions.
Leonardo da Vinci 1452–1519

It's so important to help children to think well for themselves. How we think about things has an enormous effect on our life and how we live it. My dictionary defines 'thinker' as 'a person with a skilled or powerful mind'. It's essential that children become thinkers. In every area of their lives it is crucial that children can think, make informed opinions, be able to consider carefully and produce original ideas.

For something that is so important, we often overlook or take thinking for granted. It's as if it is just like breathing, or something we simply do automatically. However, in reality, to be a good and effective thinker takes practice and, paradoxically, thought.

Children are always trying to understand about the world by questioning, by putting names to things, by seeking to find out more, by making links and connections and discovering differences. Our children need to think to learn, and learn to think. We need to value their thinking and questioning and celebrate their efforts to understand.

Children need to be able to open up the 'computer file' in their heads and collect any relevant information gathered in the past. They need to be able to bring back and brainstorm knowledge or experiences to apply these ideas to a new example or situation. Yesterday's knowledge and experience is not finished with and forgotten. It can be reinvented, recycled and enriched to build a better idea today.

When children are confronted with a problem or something they have to do, they can work out the right strategy by reflecting on past experiences. They can work out a plan, talk to themselves and say, 'I don't really need to do this to do that, I could … instead'. 'Gee I'd better slow down', or 'I'll never do it this way again'.

When you chase ideas with children, talk about where you got your ideas and questions from. Also discuss how you arrived at your answer, the alternatives that ran through your mind, and why you chose a specific answer. Be aware of the links and connections you made. Next time you have a similar problem or issue to solve, you will have some strategies to help to tackle it, to make decisions and to plan a course of action.

Chasing ideas is thinking out loud

Adults are constantly chasing ideas and thinking aloud. When we're confronted with a task or problem, we work out strategies and reflect on our plans. We talk to ourselves as we go along, saying things like, 'This isn't working!' 'I should have …', 'I'll never do that again!' or 'Next time I'll …'. When we do this we are being aware of thinking.

I can remember being told as a girl, 'Talking to yourself is the first sign of madness.' What rubbish! Chasing ideas helps us to sort out our thoughts and reflect about our thinking. When I talk to myself I discover all manner of new issues. Self-talk plays a vital role in helping us to focus and to concentrate on the issue. It helps us identify goals or outcomes, to see where we are heading; it helps us to sort and classify, to break down and arrange issues into manageable bits.

> Awareness of your own thinking – your self-talk – is called *metacognition* (*meta*: about; *cog*: thinking). Reflective people question, self-question and link ideas to experiences they have had before.

In a similar way, when we talk to family and friends we are chasing ideas and thinking out loud – bringing our ideas out into the light of day to examine them more carefully.

Question yourself

This reflective approach gives children the opportunity to see into your mind when you think aloud. Wonder 'What if …?' 'How do I think differently about …?' 'What should I do next? Why?' 'Why did I think that …?' to give them examples of how you think and how you do things.

Question yourself, question ideas, look for patterns, ask all sorts of questions to pull in more knowledge. Stimulate your thinking with questions and look for the thinking strategies you can use. By asking yourself questions you will understand how you reach conclusions.

Step by step

Recognise the steps and strategies you use to solve problems or accomplish tasks. For example if your child asks you 'How did you cook dinner?', rather than saying 'I just did it!' you could reflect back on the steps you took: 'I had planned to have roast lamb for dinner tonight. When I was shopping I bought the roast, the vegetables and this afternoon I smothered the joint in garlic, rosemary and added salt and pepper, then put the roast in the oven while I prepared the vegetables … When I was peeling the potatoes I told myself to put potatoes on the shopping list … then I …'

There are many different steps and ways of arriving at an answer. If you ask a group of people, 'What is half of ten plus ten?' you might get two completely different answers. Some people in the group might answer 'ten', others might answer 'fifteen'.

When asked how they worked out the answer, people might reply in three different ways:

* 'I just knew' or 'I just did it'. These replies don't shed any light on how they arrived at their answer. 'Just knowing' is not going to help us work out why there were two different answers to a simple problem. 'Just did it' will not help someone else solve a similar problem.
* 'I added ten and ten and got twenty, then I divided twenty by two and got the answer ten.'
* 'I halved ten to make five, then I added ten and got the answer fifteen' (using the mathematical rule of BODMAS – Brackets Of Division Multiplication Addition Subtraction, that acknowledges some signs are processed before others).

> If we change the ways we make decisions we change the decisions we make.

Reflecting on how *you* did the sum is important. Reflective answers would show *how you* arrived at your conclusion. Your knowledge of mathematics and how you approached the problem will determine how you arrived at the answer. You can use this knowledge to solve other mathematical problems.

Far-fetched connections

Finding far-fetched connections provides another way to help you *reflect* and find our what made you think of a certain idea, or the steps that helped you reach your conclusion. If you try to find connections or relationships between things that at first glance do not appear to have any similarities, you focus intently on the characteristics or qualities of the thing. If you are forced to 'invent' connections, creative and critical thinking is brought to the fore, especially when you have to explain your invention.

For example, ask your child, 'Why are you like a pencil?' They might reply, 'I'm like a pencil because I'm tall and thin, I'm colourful, I'm useful, I go on and on, I take note of things, I can break, I can get lost, I'm helpful, I run out.' Your child has thought of characteristics of a pencil – its shape, what it does, what can happen to it – and linked these ideas to themselves.

It's great fun to play the Far-fetched Connection Thinking Game. What things are like a sponge? A piece of bread (it is spongy), cheese (it has holes), your mind (it absorbs things). What things are like a lemon? Yellow-coloured things like a flower, or rounded things like a ball, or sour things like vinegar or a sour person. You can think of dozens of objects for playing the Far-fetched Connection Thinking Game.

Questions without a proper answer

Ask children, 'Are you a Sun or Moon Person?' They will be intrigued. This sounds like a question without an answer. How can you answer a question that appears silly? They can think about characteristics of the sun and the moon (the sun is hot and powerful, the moon is romantic and beautiful) then try to figure out if they are more like the sun or the moon.

Ask your children to compare themselves with the sun or the moon. Some of the reasons they may give include:

* I am like the sun because I'm happy, cheerful, hot, bright, I have a hot temper, I'm active, I have blind spots like sunspots, I don't change, I affect others, I can hurt others (the sun burns).
* I am like the moon because I have a face, people see me in different ways, I shine, I'm lazy (the moon moves slowly like me), I'm romantic, I'm sensitive, I'm dark with secrets, I'm shy, I like mystery, I think more at night, I'm peaceful, silent, I brighten up peoples lives, I change a lot, my moods change, I have a hidden effect on people (like the moon on the tides), I'm a lunatic (I often feel excited and crazy at night), I hide things.

When your children have answered this 'question-without-a-proper-answer' get them to try to work out the step-by-step strategies they used. Reflect on these strategies. Discuss how your children worked out what to say. What did they say to themselves? What was their self-talk? Perhaps their reasons would include:

* I tried – even though at first it made no sense. I talked about the question and tried to get some ideas.
* I talked to myself and asked myself, 'What are some of the characteristics of the sun, and some of the characteristics of the moon?'
* I tried to focus on what I knew, what I'd remembered about the sun and the moon. I then asked myself, 'How am I similar to the sun? How am I similar to the moon?'
* I asked Mum/Dad some more questions to try to find out more about what I am meant to do.
* I then compared myself to the qualities of the sun and the moon. I worked out that I had four reasons why I was like the sun, and seven reasons why I was like the moon. Therefore I was more a moon person. If I had discovered three reasons why I was like the sun, and three reasons why I was like the moon, and none of the reasons seemed to be overpoweringly important, I would say I am a sun *and* a moon person.

Thinking and chasing ideas is a complicated process. We need to think critically – to examine, organise and reason; and to think creatively –

to formulate new ideas, to explore options and examine assumptions. When we think we imagine, remember, arrange, define, interpret, predict, translate, clarify, solve, examine, calculate, demonstrate, classify, compare, contrast, predict, plan, create, combine, propose, decide, judge and justify. It is like a workout for the mind.

Choose your words

To chase ideas effectively, both you and others need to understand what you're saying. Try to choose your words carefully. Don't say, 'You know, kind of like' or 'Like, weird stuff', 'You know, everybody has one', 'You know what I mean!'. Help your children to be more specific when they are expressing an idea. Reword and repeat their idea back to them and say, 'Do you mean that …' and discuss another way you could explain the idea. By giving an example of the issue, you can together fine-tune the idea so that someone can easily understand it.

Be aware of vocabulary that can express ideas more precisely. Help children grow their vocabulary so that they can distinguish the meanings of words and find the word that is just right.

Think things through

Ponder and think things through. Even if you think you know all about the idea, set an example, and talk about other approaches to the issue. If your children jump into a discussion boots first, remind them how you need to play with ideas and think things over. Give them a couple of examples. Remember the discussion about 'What sank the *Titanic*?'.

Let your children simplify issues in a complex idea. Show them how to find complexities in what appears at first glance to be a simple idea, and encourage them to think in a flexible way. Help them to be more aware of the importance of thinking things through by showing them alternative approaches to ideas.

Use humour

When you are fine-tuning an idea, be humorous and outrageous. Misunderstand your child's idea or word. Be humorous with homonyms (words that sound the same but have different meanings). For example when you child uses the word 'right', meaning okay, pretend to be puzzled because you think they mean the opposite of left. Be amusing when you play devil's advocate, find examples or counter examples. Fool around with the idea with your children, tell outrageous, obvious fibs, exaggerate, role play, act, tell jokes about the topic or idea, make puns and have fun.

> Be ingenious, original and insightful to unlock your children's creativity.

Use all your senses

Show your children how to use as many senses as they can when they are gathering information. The more senses engaged in the process, the more pathways to the brain are opened.

Look at a picture, read something, talk about it, feel an object. Colours, textures and patterns, music, rhyme, humour, and words all speak to us.

Be persistent

We need to demonstrate perseverance when we're thinking about a puzzle or problem. Children should learn the habit of perseverance when the solution to a problem is not immediately apparent.

We ought to show children that sometimes we need to have not only a Plan A, but also a Plan B, a Plan C and maybe even a Plan D. In other words if the first plan does not work – try something else. If that does not work you may need to keep trying different ideas until you can find a solution. Rethinking your aim may be necessary. The message to give your children is that with perseverance and creativity you can come to an improved understanding about a problem.

Have you heard the saying that the word 'triumph' is made up of two words, 'try' and 'umph'? Our children need to be motivated to try, and to put a lot of effort into trying.

Record it!

Write down the thoughts of the moment. Those that come unsought for are commonly the most valuable.

Francis Bacon 1561–1626

We need to pay attention to what children say. Recording their ideas demonstrates that we are treating what they say thoughtfully and seriously. Imagine the boost to their self-esteem when you say, 'Hang on a minute, that's a fantastic thought. I'll just write it down so we won't forget it!'

Record all sorts of things: things your child really loves or is curious about, favourite colours, new words they use, a diary of adventure or finding-out days, when you set out to explore certain things.

Granddaughter Lucinda, aged two, is fascinated by the whole concept of water. Her father took her on a 'water tour' to see all the fountains, ponds and water walls in the city. He even took her to the thirty-fifth floor of a city building to see the view overlooking both the river and the bay. When he repeats the exercise when Lucinda is a little older, imagine the language learning that will take place on such a fun day out. How interesting to capture some of the things Lucinda said to her dad – some of her observations and comments. Walking into a shopping mall recently, she said to me, 'Nanny, I can smell dancing water!'. She recognised the smell of chlorine in a fountain!

Keeping a record of your children's thoughts is invaluable.

Thinking Trap Resource Book

Purchase an exercise book to be your Thinking Trap Resource Book – somewhere to trap your thoughts. You will find it helpful to jot down the thoughts and ideas that emerge when you and your children are talking.

Record your discoveries, your thoughts, your plans, your goals. Your Thinking Trap Resource Book will provide you with a record of your ideas to refer back to, and to add to, and you will be able to observe the growth of understanding. By recording goals and plans you will then have ideas to work on.

Writing down goals is an important thing to do.

In 1954, students at Yale University were asked the question, 'Do you have goals?'. Ten percent of the students had goals. Four percent wrote them down. In 1974 a follow up on this group of students found that the four percent who had written down their goals had achieved them compared with the other ninety-six percent.

John McBeth, 7th International Thinking Conference, Singapore, 1977

If you focus on 'What is truth?' or 'Do I see what I believe or do I believe what I see?' the action of writing something down will help you to concentrate on the concept.

Perhaps, like me, you keep a notebook next to your bed to jot down the problems you have solved in your sleep. My brain frequently has the best ideas when I am asleep, and I need to catch these ideas quickly when I wake up or I tend to forget my 'brainwaves'. Perhaps in your sleep you will visit the discussion you have been having and you will make some new connections. Trap these thoughts in your Thinking Trap Resource Book.

Keep thinking resources. Collect interesting, quirky, strange, thought-provoking, funny or crazy cuttings from newspapers or photocopied pages of books, or simply an idea jotted down on a piece of paper, in the back of your Thinking Trap Resource Book.

Your thinking resources can include newspaper cartoons and notes about television programs, movies and other things that you know will interest your children. Keep a special eye open for anything to do with animals or your children's particular passions. If they are crazy about horses, whales, dogs or actors, find snippets of news about these topics that have ideas about fairness, cheating, fame, privacy, animal rights or rights of the individual – or even styles of clothing to discuss.

The purpose of each article you collect is to whet the curiosity of your children.

Pearls of Wisdom Book

Buy an attractive book with blank or lined pages to become your Pearls of Wisdom Book. When your children make a comment that is interesting, record their gems of wit and wisdom. You might want to have an individual book for each of your children. These records will make a unique gift to present to your child for their twenty-first birthday. Record and date their comments in your book. You can use their statements as a discussion starter at a later time. Don't forget to record some of your own discoveries and share these with your child.

You might like to organise your Pearls of Wisdom Book by starting each idea with the words 'I've discovered that'. I talk with young students at school about all sorts of things. They share their ideas. I record them. I simply add, 'I've discovered that' when I read their discoveries back to them. It doesn't take them long to copy my example and start their sentences with 'I've discovered'.

I've discovered

Six-year-olds: I've discovered that a rabbit can be a pet ... that the tooth fairy is real because she leaves glitter footprints ... that books help you discover things ... that I've still got my baby teeth but I'm not a baby.

Seven-year-olds: I've discovered that people don't always like the same thing ... that when you're little you can think there's a robber under the bed ... that grown-ups can tell fibs ... that it's hard to know if the truth is true.

Eight-year-olds: I've discovered that I'm quiet but I think a lot ... that you can't always get what you want ... that most people are more attractive with hair ... that love is nicer than just liking.

Nine-year-olds: I've discovered that reading a book is easier than writing one ... that you shouldn't treat animals as toys ... that people don't always take jokes as jokes ... that ideas are contagious.

Ten-year-olds: I've discovered that old people want to be young and young people want to be old ... that dreams can come from books and the reverse ... that when I go to bed I don't remember going to sleep.

Eleven-year-olds: I've discovered that when you copy it is a compliment ... that sometimes if you want to keep a friend you try to do everything the same ... that your thoughts can keep you company. When you've got an empty head you're lonely ... it's interesting to watch how people treat each other.

At the end of a chasing ideas session you might make an 'I've discovered that' statement to summarise what conclusions you have reached. It will not be long before your children start to make up their own discoveries for you to record. Initially you may need to help them translate their notion by listening to them very carefully and then saying 'Do you mean that ...?'.

Here are some discoveries from my students. Each discovery has been made by thinking, making connections, reasoning and judging. These are perfect examples of chasing ideas – children trying to understand the world and how it relates to them.

Some of your children's Pearls of Wisdom may be conclusions from a discussion; others may be from a note you jotted down when your child made an interesting statement. My daughter Andrea has started recording little gems from things her daughter Lucinda says.

Make use of every happening: birthdays, school camps, holidays or travel to record some discoveries. For instance if your child has been acting in the school play you could ask them what they have learnt about themselves in the process. Some ten-year-olds I know learnt from being in a play that most mistakes aren't noticed, that parents can embarrass you and that if you run up and down and squeeze someone's arm it helps your nerves!

Recorded thoughts and ideas are concrete proof to your children that they are indeed great thinkers!

By recording their thoughts, you will encourage children to be aware and to be confident thinkers.

Develop an encouraging environment

Encouragement has been extremely important in my life. In my book *Doing Up Buttons* I tell of my struggle to put my life together after my terrible car accident a decade ago. A man failing to stop at a Stop sign hit the rear passenger side of my car, which spun my car around. A power pole in the driver's door stopped the car and stopped me too. I would not have coped without love and encouragement from my family.

My husband and children each had their own unique way of encouraging me. Husband Ted did everything in his power to help me deal with the terrible pain. Helen would try to divert me and make suggestions to help me cope mentally. Andrea would hover in the background, making dressing and coping a little easier with her thoughtfulness. Ken would act as a kindly chauffeur, making the endless rounds of doctor's visits more bearable. Rob on the other hand would pat me when I wept with pain and frustration, and when my life seemed just too hard. It's amazing how encouraging a pat can be.

My father was particularly helpful in encouraging me to accept and tackle my situation as a challenge. We had many wonderful philosophical discussions about life. He enjoyed telling me stories of his childhood. His stories helped me to accept my pain, double vision and tremendous difficulty with my memory and understanding. His stories gave me hope for the future. There was the time his grandfather had said, 'Markie, we are all just like ants on a summer's day.' Dad, at the tender age of five, had no idea what the words meant (expressing the brevity of man's existence and his insignificance in a boundless universe) but the way his grandfather treated him like a 'person' left a lasting memory.

Dad was always keen to discuss my work at school and my lessons. He'd add suggestions, and school day and 'teacher stories' would follow. His earliest school days were sweetened by the words of encouragement of Miss Grey his teacher when she'd praised his plasticine 'sparrow'. He had the pleasure of helping her with a hearing aid when she was an old lady and discovered that she regarded encouragement as the greatest gift a teacher could have.

> Praise and encouragement are the greatest gifts.

Encouragement was at the heart of another story. On a cold grey day (when I was a year old) Dad was wandering round the grounds of the institution made famous by Helen Keller in the United States when he was invited to observe a young lady teaching a sweet little girl who was deaf and blind. When he was leaving, he tried to express some of his emotion and admiration. To his surprise the teacher burst into tears. She was on the point of giving up. She spoke of discouragement and the slowness of results. Dad's visit had renewed her spirit. The weather was even more dismal when he left the building but he felt he was walking on air. 'Chick, we can never know the importance of words of encouragement,' he would say.

> We can never know the importance of words of encouragement.

Dad was constantly speaking about the great need people have for appreciation, approbation and encouragement. Encouragement has been a strong thread, like gold, woven through my life. Encouragement has helped me to cope. Encouragement can help your children to cope; encouragement from your children can help you cope.

Handy Thinking keys and tools

5

> *Hercule Poirot tapped his forehead. 'These little grey cells,*
> *it is "up to them" as you say over here.'*
>
> Agatha Christie 1891–1975

To chase ideas with children, you need something to talk about. You need to find an idea or an issue to discuss with them.

Keys to unlock minds

Stories, objects and happenings can all be used to tease and tantalise your children to chase ideas and to think more. These are like a key that will unlock their minds. In this book you'll find a wide range of entertaining and thought-provoking keys. After you have tried some of these keys you will soon discover your own keys to use with your children.

Remember that just about anything can be used as a key to unlock their thoughts or as a starting point to open up their minds to think about topics or issues. You may have already started collecting interesting snippets from magazines or newspapers to stick in the back of your Thinking Trap Resource Book.

Five important thinking tools for finding ideas

Once you have found something to discuss, you need tools to help you to open up all the issues connected with it. The five thinking tools will help you to chase ideas and unpack issues so that you will focus on each issue and understand more about it. By linking the issue to things you already know, by finding similarities and differences, and by making comparisons and trying to fit the idea being discussed with other ideas, your children will learn valuable thinking skills to apply in other situations. They will also learn to concentrate and focus, to listen carefully and to communicate thoughtfully.

Thinking tools to further unlock concepts include Pigeonhole It, Find the Facts, Find the Feelings, Good, Bad and Curious, and What If ...?

1. Pigeonhole It

This tool helps you to sort, organise and group ideas and things. To solve problems, make plans, understand an issue or comprehend an idea, children need to be able to focus on it and analyse some of the components of it. Whether focusing on an idea, an object or a problem, it's very helpful to find out whether this idea is similar to something you're familiar with and why you think this is so. Make comparisons and find connections to help you classify ideas with other similar ideas, objects with things that have similarities, or problems that are like other problems. This will help you classify or put the idea or object in a pigeonhole, with other similar ideas or objects. By asking, 'What is it like?', you reflect on it, analyse and make decisions.

To Pigeonhole It, you need to do oodles of evaluating and judging to look at similarities and differences. The significant thing about Pigeonholing It is that sometimes the pigeon (or idea) is in one hole, at other times – because of different ways you can classify – the idea can belong with a different set of criteria. So practicing adapting or finding new relationships or links improves our children's ability to transfer and adapt information.

You need to be perceptive and thoughtful to classify or pigeonhole something. Be observant, creative and reflective. Ask questions and really think about things to judge the best way to classify something.

To Pigeonhole It you need to judge which of the characteristics are more important.

For example, try to classify people into short or tall. Where do you draw the line? How do you define 'short' or 'tall'? Is it all relative to the group you are comparing with? In a group of basketballers, would a person of average height look short?

Pigeonholing It requires reflective thought, analysis and decision-making.

When there has been a big event in your life, or children have been arguing about who gets the bigger piece of cake, use the cake as a key to open up their minds. Use the Pigeonhole It game to open up the issue of 'bigness'. Examine the notion of 'big' – in importance, in size, when compared with other, similar things and so forth.

What's the biggest thing there is?

Space	Ego	Giant worm	Friendship
Love	Whales	World	Stress
Skyscrapers	Mount Everest	Thinking	Ideas
Population	Moon	Ocean	The future ...

(For more examples of Pigeonhole It, see pages 68–70 and Chapter 10.)

2. Find the Facts

The facts are always important. Whatever idea you are examining, brainstorm issues by trying to find the facts. Do not make assumptions, read between the lines or put your own perspective on the issue when you are doing this sort of thinking. It is quite tricky to accurately retell the facts. Finding ideas this way is not creative, it is simply trying to report the facts.

Discuss a film you have seen together, or a news report or an article in a newspaper or magazine you have read with your children. Point out all the *facts* in the article.

(For some examples of Find the Facts thinking see pages 70, 100–104 and 116.)

3. Find the Feelings

This type of insightful, creative thinking is very different from Find the Facts thinking. Try to see the issue from several points of view. Find the Feelings is important as it allows children to empathise with others and to appreciate the role of emotions in thinking. Discuss how you and your children feel about an issue, how you'd feel if you were the main character in the story, a friend of that character, or a bystander. Try to see the issue from several points of view. This is creative thinking.

As an example, use the Find the Feelings tool to discuss the feelings behind crying when you have seen someone cry. Why do people cry? Classify all the reasons you can think of.

Because they are happy
Because they are sad
Because their feelings are hurt
Because they have hurt their body
Because they are sick
Because they are embarrassed
Because they're feeling left out
Because someone they know dies or a pet dies or is lost
Because they're scared
Because they're jealous, lonely, guilty
Because they're really angry about something or someone
Because they're spoilt and they haven't got their own way

Because a film was sad, happy, romantic, touching

Because someone they like is leaving to live somewhere else

(For more examples of Find the Feelings thinking see pages 70, 100–104.)

4. Good, Bad and Curious

This is creative, reflective, questioning, critical thinking. You are detectives looking for Good things, Bad things and Curious things about an issue or topic. Note that your comments about Curious things will nearly always be questions. For example, 'How come it was okay for …?' 'Why did …?' 'What would happen if …?' 'Does this mean that …?' 'If … would that make a difference?'

If your children complain about having to wear a school uniform, or you are buying new uniforms, use this as a key to open up their minds to wonder about uniforms. Use the Good, Bad and Curious tool to open up the issue.

Good

☑ Everybody is dressed the same
☑ Pupils feel like they belong
☑ Cuts out competition between children wearing expensive label clothes or lots of different clothes to impress
☑ Practical
☑ Easy to know what to wear
☑ Saves fights with your mum over what to wear
☑ Easy to report back to the school if pupils are seen acting badly
☑ Easy to hand down clothes
☑ Can buy second-hand uniforms

Bad

✗ Expensive
✗ Jumpers can be itchy
✗ Sometimes they are uncomfortable
✗ Sometimes they are too hot or too cold for the weather
✗ They don't express your individuality

Curious

？ Why does a uniform make an impact?

? Do clothes make an impact?
? Is fashion important?
? Do people judge you by how you dress?
? Are the colours of a uniform important?
? Is a uniform a symbol?
? Should all schools have uniforms?
? Uniforms need to be worn neatly … how strict should it be?

(For more examples of Good, Bad and Curious thinking see pages 70–72, 74–75 and Chapter 11.)

5. What If …?

This thinking tool requires creative, reflective, questioning and critical thinking. Ask the question 'What If …?' to think about consequences. What if an element of the story were changed? Predict the outcomes, be aware of the influence of assumptions, look at cause and effect and give reasons for opinions. This thinking tool is very useful in a wide variety of instances.

If there is a news report about people lost at sea, in the desert, or in the snow, ask some 'What If …?' questions.

What if people were forced to take a beeper/mobile phone/flare when they are going off the beaten track?

What if people who had been rescued from a dangerous situation at sea or in the desert had to invent something that would help others in a similar situation?

What if there were rules for people going out into the wilderness?

What if character A did XYZ in the movie we just saw?

What if we all were magic?

What if people who do kind deeds were always rewarded?

(For more examples of What If …? thinking see pages 75, 136.)

Use the five thinking tools – the Handy Way

As you have seen, there are five important thinking tools to help you unpack issues when you're chasing ideas. The digits on your hand can represent each of these thinking tools. Once your children become adept at using these tools, they will always have at their fingertips

> Thinking the Handy Way about any topic opens up the subject and lets you focus on different issues.

powerful tools to help them examine and tackle issues and problems. They may be lost for words for a moment, but they will never forget that they have these helpful tools to help them – they simply look at their fingers as a reminder.

Your thumb is a very useful digit. You need to use your thumb to grasp things. You can't give things the 'thumbs up' or 'thumbs down' until you start to grasp the issues and classify the object or idea, or Pigeonhole It. Ask yourself, 'What is it like?' to grasp how the concept or idea fits into some form of classification.

Your pointer finger points you to Find the Facts. You have to take the facts into account whenever you have a discussion.

Your middle finger stands for things that are in the middle or at the heart of the issue. Find the Feelings leads to empathetic thinking. With this tool you are trying to find out why you feel the way you do, or what other people's feelings about the issue might be.

Your ring finger is associated with rings. A ring is a whole circle; it also has a hole in the middle. To look at the whole subject you need to look at the Good, Bad and Curious issues.

Your little finger we will call the What If …? finger. It stands for the What If …? thinking, where we wonder, 'What if we changed …?'.

Example: Think the Handy Way about horse racing

1. Pigeonhole It: What other things are like horse racing? Greyhound racing, pigeon racing, the trots, chariot racing, jousting on horseback, fox hunting, dressage (competing on good looks rather than speed) equestrian events, polo, running races, Olympic events.

2. Find the Facts: what are some facts about horse racing? First horse past the post wins, horse must have a jockey on its back, see who can win the race, trainer/owner can get a lot of money, some people like to bet which horse will win, some people make lots of money betting, some people lose lots of money betting, some women go to horse races to look elegant and fashionable, some horses hurt themselves and have to be put down, some people cheat by giving their horse drugs, horses are tested for drugs.

3. Find the Feelings: What are some of the feelings associated with horse racing? Excitement, love the races, fun, feel sorry for the animals, feel it is cruel as horses are sometimes whipped, happy for the horses because they are well fed and looked after, sad about people who lose money betting, great for people who have won money.

4. Good, Bad and Curious: We have mentioned Good and Bad points already; what is Curious about horse racing? Do horses have the choice whether they run fast or not? Do the horses enjoy racing? Would it be better to be a wild horse or a racing horse? Why are horses put down when they break their legs? How are horses treated if they win? If they lose? Is it hard to be a jockey? Is it fair that the jockeys have to be a certain weight? Should people gamble? Is gambling wrong? Why do people gamble?

5. What If …?: What if racing were banned? What if it were illegal to gamble? What if hurt horses were left to live? What if the jockeys were not allowed to whip the horses? What if more people owned race horses? What if people raced donkeys, or elephants instead? What if we owned a race horse?

> ### Getting started
> * When you are playing with ideas with your children treat it as a game, a fun thing that you can do together
> * Start in a small way and build from there
> * Don't emphasise getting into deep and meaningful discussions too early
> * It takes practice and time to develop your own way to use these tools

Acronyms and abbreviations to make it fun

You can use acronyms to create the element of play rather than 'hard serious stuff'. Add a secret society atmosphere to your praise by saying, maybe with a secret wink, that an idea is a VIP (Very Important Proposition) or GST (Good Sound Thinking). If your children have suggested something that is wrong, soften your criticism or correction of their thoughts by suggesting that it is NQR (Not Quite Right).

Compliment or praise a specific thought by calling it IT (Insightful Thinking – about others) or ET (Enhanced Thinking – where your child has demonstrated they can use lots of thinking strategies to express an idea).

You might enjoy using Salman Rushdie's 'P2C2E' (Process Too Complicated to Explain) when ideas are very complicated, or 'SEP' (Someone Else's Problem) from Douglas Adams' *The Hitchhikers Guide to the Galaxy*. What about 'R2D2' to mean 'I'm ready to deliver to you my idea'? Use your imagination and have fun. Praise your child every day with abbreviations.

Days of the Square Table

Our children always ended up having big discussions at mealtimes. Ken said, 'We're just like King Arthur and his knights of the round table.' Our table is square so the kids suggested that we call ourselves Mum and her Days (opposite of nights!) of the Square Table. This they shortened to 'Days' – a fierce competition to find acronyms ensued. Acronyms included 'Dazzling Accomplished Yakking Succeeders', 'Destined Achieving Yielding Spirits', 'Daring Alert Young Sensations' … never before have I seen kids fight to use the dictionary!

What does being sensible mean?
Children pigeonhole some advice

* Remember that others can see what we think is hidden
* The feelings we have on the inside can be different to the feelings we show on the outside
* Jealousy can poison you
* Don't judge a book by its cover
* Make the most of life
* You can't always see what is true
* Don't be afraid to take calculated risks (after you've thought carefully about the risks and looked at the good, bad and curious issues)
* Always have a Plan B
* Follow your dreams
* Look at the glass as half full rather than half empty
* Think before you act
* Have fun
* Trust your own ideas
* Don't spend your life crying – forgive people and get on with life
* Life is too short to be little
* Things are worth it (effort and even pain) in the end – this includes braces on your teeth
* Be brave
* Remember teasing can sometimes go too far!
* Be a loyal friend
* Don't be afraid to work to make things happen
* Knowledge is power
* Remember you have dignity and rights as a human being
* Anything is possible; pigs can fly!

Creating the atmosphere

Do what you can, with what you have, where you are.

Theodore Roosevelt 1858–1919

Improve your communication with your children by entering their world. When you embark on thinking adventures with your children you will be starting within their comfort zone of the ordinary and concrete, and you will gradually push out that comfort zone to discuss curious, interesting and important issues with them. While doing this stretching, you will be actively enjoying their company and the time you spend together.

Enter their world

The valuable time you spend with your children is not the intense 'I've dropped everything for you, Darling, now we are going to have some quality time (whether you want it or not!)'. It's the friendly, casual, everyday making and taking opportunities when the time is right. Enter their world by wondering aloud with them at mealtimes, walking, cooking, gardening, bath time, brushing the dog, waiting at the doctor's, driving to school and sports, brushing hair, combing their hair for nits – the list of available time for wondering is endless.

Chasing ideas and playing with them should fit in with what you are doing. Grab any opportunity while you are washing, walking or waiting.

Find and share

Each day, look for something interesting or beautiful to share with your children. It may be a feather, a flock of birds against a blue sky, a perfect autumn leaf or a spider's web holding dewdrops. Get your children to drag you outside to show you something they have seen. Show them your appreciation. Tell them that you would have missed seeing that beetle or cloud if they hadn't shown it to you.

Tell them about the book you are reading, maybe even read them a paragraph and explain how the topic made you think of them. Share something you saw in a movie, a play or a television program with them.

> You need to show your children that you will listen, that you think they are clever, that you have faith in them, that you have time to enter their world.

Sharing does not have to be a long, detailed and drawn-out process, but just a casual brief encounter of minds. When children share their ideas with you, be interested but don't grill them or dig in too deeply.

Explain that you are going to share ideas and thoughts, discuss all sorts of things, talk about things you don't usually notice, look at things from different angles and think harder. By using special thinking magnifying glasses to help focus more carefully, special thinking binoculars to see into the distance and the future, special thinking x-rays to see beneath the surface and read between the lines, you will become detectives, journalists, storytellers, magicians and judges.

When introducing children to the notion of starting to look at the world with new eyes, there are a few stories, tricks and games that will help them to 'see' differently. Tell the following story to your children:

The strong men story

Imagine a Strong Man show. Gathered on stage were the strongest men in the world, muscles bulging and gleaming. The competition had been fierce between the men, each man straining to show he was the strongest. Then the compere threw a challenge to the audience; he asked if there was anyone who could tear a pile of telephone books in half, with their bare hands. There was silence. Then a small boy in the back row put up his hand. He stood and walked down the aisle while the 'strong men' on the stage sniggered. The small boy walked up to the pile of telephone books, and taking the first book, commenced tearing the book in half, page by page.

'If you do someting wrong it isn't the end of the world!'
Sam (aged nine)
'You can solve anything if you put your mind to it.'
Hayley (aged ten)

This story has several messages for children. You can't judge a book by its cover; the strong men thought that he was just a weedy little kid, but that boy had hidden mind strength! There's more than one way of skinning a cat; if you use your brains you will think of things other people haven't even considered. That courage is important; imagine how nervous the boy must have felt … but he did it! And also one of my favourite sayings is that triumph is made up of two words: 'try' and 'umph'!

The two faces

We all see things in certain ways. We can all look at the same thing yet see different things. There is a very old drawing that helps demonstrate this. Show one child the first illustration of a woman's head and another child the second illustration of a woman's head (on pages 48–49).

Make sure that they are concentrating, and point out a couple of obvious things – 'You see a picture of a lady … it's up to you to decide if she is young or old … you can see she has a sort of scarf on her head'. Get the children to take a 'photo' of the sketch in their minds.

Put those two illustrations down and show them both the third one. Ask them, 'Is it a young lady or an old lady?' As your children start to argue as to whether she is young or old, explain that you have tricked them – the picture shows both a young and an old lady. Then show them the first and second illustrations and explain how you had 'brainwashed' them to see the lady as young or old.

> 'There is no limit to your imagination'.
> Labrini (aged eleven)
> 'If you have a problem, blaming and hurting others doesn't help. It just makes other people suffer as well.'
> Will (aged eleven)

Now is the time to explain that frequently there is more than one 'right' answer, and we need to remember everyone sees things differently. Perhaps at some future date, when a mighty argument is brewing, the words 'It's just like the two ladies' will remind your children that we all see things differently.

The marshmallows and chopsticks game

Place the contents of a packet of marshmallows on a plate on the table and tell your children they can eat as many as they like as long as they obey the rules of the game. With left arms behind their backs and right arms outstretched, wrap a newspaper round their right arms to form a tube to stop the arm bending. Then tape the tube. Place a chopstick in the right hand and watch the frustration! How long will it take for it

to dawn on them that they cannot feed themselves … but they can feed each other?

Use this little game to point out that if we use our heads we can do all sorts of things we might have thought were impossible. It is also a good way to explain that when we chase ideas we are going to cooperate and help each other to get to the reward of understanding.

Crack the code

To help children understand that they need to look at things and think about things in a special way you could try this old mind-reading party trick. Tell them you have developed mental telepathy between you and one of your children; they can read your mind and you can pass on messages about certain chosen objects.

Before presenting this trick, talk privately to one child (they will be your assistant) and choose a colour or a surface (such as wood) that will be the code to indicate that the next object you touch is the chosen one.

Then explain to the rest of the family that you have discovered this 'gift' of mental telepathy. Your assistant will go outside the room and shut the door while the rest of the family chooses an object. When your assistant returns to the room, point to an object and ask if this is the chosen one: 'No', point to another object, 'No', another and another,

'No', then point to the agreed code, something black or something wooden for example. Now point at the chosen object, 'Yes.'

This trick is sure to get their brains ticking over! There will be loads of suggestions about how you do it, and of course you can repeat the trick time and again. You can let the family in on the fact that it's really a trick and get the children to observe very carefully each time. Eventually, the other children will 'see' your code and in the process will have concentrated very hard, made hypotheses, and acted like detectives and judges.

Be explorers, detectives, magicians and judges

Find things out by tentatively probing ideas and feelings. Fumble for hints and explanations. Read between the lines.

One of my early memories is amazingly vivid. I was quite small and I'd gone to the letterbox to get the letters when I saw tiny 'creatures' dancing in the sunlight. I'd never noticed these creatures before, and I was so excited because here, in the ordinary everyday air, was something that until that moment had been hidden.

As I was wrapped up in fairies at the time, and I was searching madly for 'proof' that they were real, I spent several golden days believing these tiny things were real fairies floating and flying and twirling. I can remember the excitement of lying in bed and watching them twirl, entranced and mystified and feeling chuffed that the little folk had let me into their secret world.

It didn't take long for realisation to rear its ugly head. If the air was so thick with fairies how come you didn't (gulp) swallow them? If all the air was stuffed full of fairies, that would be just too many fairies, wouldn't it?

They had followed me from the letterbox to my room but maybe this was not a flock of fairies following me round, maybe the air was always full of swirling mites. It was just the sunlight that had let me see the invisible drifting dust. Aha, now I was getting somewhere; just as the invisible ink of lemon juice could become visible, so things could appear and disappear.

I knew that I couldn't believe my eyes because on many occasions when I'd lost something, a sock or a pencil, I'd search and couldn't see it. But Mum could always find it, right under my nose! How come my eyes didn't work properly?

Discovering the 'truth' about the swirling dust mites meant that I had 'cut my teeth' as a detective. I'd solved a mystery all on my own.

I also felt like a genuine magician. I'd pulled invisible ideas out of the box, so to speak. Just as I had watched in amazement as a magician showed the audience a large empty box, then pulled smaller boxes out of it, or a string of silk scarves out of someone's ear, I had pulled ideas out of other ideas, and discovered ideas where I never thought ideas would be.

I felt a constant challenge to try to discover scraps of hidden information, odds and ends from the invisible world of 'truth', facts from the grown-up world. I'd pick up clues, or snatches of 'truth' from conversations, lyrics of songs and by looking at things. I'd share lots of my discoveries with Dad. It was so exciting to try to discover the huge, hidden secret world of ideas that really ruled the world.

Each day became the scene for a new treasure hunt where there'd be ideas or 'truth', hidden in everyday life. These ideas were just waiting for me, the explorer, the detective and the judge to uncover.

These ideas were more than imagination because they were 'real'!

Discovering these unknown clues about life, imagination, adventure, magic, mystery, beliefs and priorities gave me a sense of achievement and pride. It also forged bonds of understanding with Dad.

Your children need you to invest in 'blue chip' thinking with them. Catch curiosity together! Get hooked on ideas and together go fishing in the big pond of life.

Reading through your forehead

Another trick that will intrigue your family but is equally simple is the 'I can read through my forehead' trick. Once again, you need to take a child aside and explain the trick to them. Tell them to assist you by saying, with amazement, 'That was mine' after you 'read' the first piece of paper.

Explain to the family that you have found yourself possessed by another 'gift': you can read without using your eyes! Distribute pencils and slips of paper about six centimetres by three centimetres. Explain to the gang that you are going to leave the room while they determine what category of things they are going to write down – perhaps countries, cities, food, names or animals.

Your helper participates in the proceedings. When you return to the room, make sure that when you collect the papers (now folded), you put your helper's paper at the bottom of the pile.

The rest is easy and fun. Ask what category has been chosen (let's say in this instance the group chose the category of animals). After a bit of acting about 'getting the vibe', close your eyes and place the first paper on your forehead with the writing against your head. Act a little more then say, 'springbok'. Choose something unusual or someone else may have written it! Your helper looks surprised and says, 'Yes that is mine!'

Then you take the paper off your forehead, read it (this gives you the next 'guess') and say, 'Yes, I was right! It *was* springbok' even though you will have read another word, such as 'elephant.' Scrunch the paper up.

Repeat the process of pretending to read with your eyes closed, paper on your forehead. You now have the next animal to pretend to mind-read: 'elephant'. If you lose the plot or get flustered just say that you've lost the gift for the moment.

If your children have not seen the trick before they will be intrigued and fascinated, and try to work out what is happening. A lot of hard thinking will happen before they discover how the trick was done.

Do our eyes/ears/mouth work?

We think our eyes, ears and mouth always work, but often they don't. Give one child a piece of paper and a pencil and ask another child to describe the following illustration, Illustration 1. The first child is to draw exactly what they are told. The 'teller' must not see what the 'drawer' is doing. When the 'drawer' has completed the drawing, compare the original with the drawing that has just been completed. Look at where they had difficulty explaining or

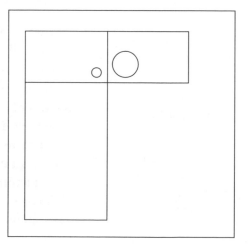

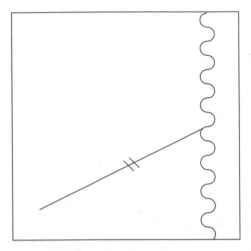

understanding directions, discuss how hard it is to get an idea out of one head and into someone else's head. Now try Illustration 2. How was the wavy line described? What is a squiggle to you might mean something totally different to me. If it is so difficult to describe something we can see, no wonder it is so hard to explain our ideas.

This is a good rainy day game, and if you play it several times (making up your own illustrations), your children will learn to speak with care and try to

be accurate in describing a design. They will understand how hard it is to communicate clearly. The 'drawer' will listen with care, having learnt how difficult it is to understand what someone is saying. When the 'teller' is making up a picture they will quickly learn to use designs they can describe.

We take it for granted that we 'tell the truth' and that we 'hear the truth', but we all have filters on our mind's eye, which means we see things in certain ways.

'I find it really hard to know what you mean and I don't think you really exactly know what I mean.'
Sally (aged nine)

'When we all think the same thing no-one does much thinking.'
Chris (aged eight)

In days gone by, some thieves would sandpaper the tips of their fingers when preparing to commit a robbery. This was to make their fingertips more sensitive to slight movements when turning the dial on a safe they were cracking. In a similar way these pictures, games and tricks should make your children more sensitive to and aware of thinking. This should prepare them for chasing ideas.

Getting the message across

Words are, of course, the most powerful drug used by mankind.

Rudyard Kipling 1865–1936

Has your child laboured over a school project, have they ruled straight margins, illustrated it neatly, and handed it in on time only to get lower marks than a scrappy looking piece of work handed in by a classmate? This is a familiar story to so many of our children. Their disappointment, frustration and queries of 'What more could I do?' and 'What do teachers want?' can be explained by comparing Bit of Biscuit thinking and Russian Salad thinking.

Bit of Biscuit thinking

To explain good thinking to your children buy a packet of teddy bear-shaped biscuits. Explain to your children that you are going to show them something that is very important to understand about thinking.

Produce your teddy bear biscuit and bite off its head. Then, as looks of amazement and curiosity flood over your children's faces, spit the decapitated head into your hand. Ask your children what is in your hand. Of course they'll say 'a bit of biscuit'. Play along a little. Ask if they are sure, and how can they tell? What type of biscuit did it come from? Explain that this head of a teddy bear biscuit stands for knowledge – something that is easily recognised as a fact. You can recognise what type of biscuit the bit came from. In the same way a teacher might recognise which book a bit of knowledge was copied from.

Now tell the Russian Salad story.

Russian Salad thinking

Barry Humphries relates in his book *More Please* a prank that he enjoyed in his student days. He would select a bus stop in the early morning, and empty a can of Russian Salad on the pavement.

As a child in the 1950s I can well remember the sophistication of a meal with a lettuce leaf cup of this gastronomic delight! It came in a small can, about the size of a can of cat food, and it contained chopped up bits of carrot, potato and peas, all swimming in mayonnaise.

After depositing the revolting-looking mess, Barry would hurry home and dress himself as a tramp, and return, reeking of alcohol, fumbling and shuffling. By this time, a large queue would have formed at the bus stop. Humphries' act would now begin. First he would eye the mess on the ground, then he'd produce a spoon from his pocket, and having wiped it carefully on a grubby sleeve, he'd kneel down and eat the Russian Salad.

This little story will tickle the fancy of your children. There's nothing they like as much as a story that involves sick! Of course the Russian Salad is an analogy for good thinking: the peas are ideas from a thing that has happened to them or their friends, the potato might represent something related to the idea that they have seen on television or in a film or read about in a book, the carrots might be ideas from a discussion they had with the next-door neighbour, or Grandma. Now comes the important part: all these ideas are mixed up and churned around not in their stomach, but in their heads. They've found connections, relationships, similarities, differences, they've judged one idea against another idea, and come up with their own theory about the topic. They are able to justify the reasons why they say what they say.

Watch the light dawning as they realise the difference between simple thinking and enhanced thinking. Simple thinking, or Bit of Biscuit thinking may be retelling knowledge straight from a book; this is the groundwork only, the starting off point. Compare this to when the child had gathered information from several sources, thought

about the data and come up with their own original thoughts. This is Russian Salad thinking or Enhanced Thinking.

Let's return to the two school projects. The neat, attractive project was simply words copied out of books (the teacher could even recognise which books they came from). The messy project was full of lots of ideas, comparisons, and discoveries about the topic. It didn't look too crash hot but it was stuffed with interesting, original thoughts.

Next time your children make a remark that is a bit ordinary, call it Bit of Biscuit thinking and suggest they do some Russian Salad thinking about the topic.

Here's an example that shows the difference between Bit of Biscuit thinking (knowledge) and Enhanced Thinking, (chock-full of peas of ideas, carrots of comparisons and classifying, potatoes of predictions, mixed up in the mayonnaise of your own thinking, judging, evaluating and criticising).

The Five Good Thinking Steps in action

(See Bloom's Taxonomy page 173)

The television show *The Brady Bunch* can be used to demonstrate the Five Good Thinking Steps.

1. Explain (knowledge): show and identify

The Brady Bunch is an old television show. It's about a family of three boys and three girls. It was a popular show in the 1960s. They wear weird clothes. (Use the Find the Facts thinking tool to describe what you see.)

2. Understand: classify and define

Each *The Brady Bunch* program shows the family finding a problem and solving it. (Use Pigeonhole It to place the show into the context of television programs.)

3. Compare: examine and contrast

The Brady Bunch is very old fashioned because of the clothes, the ideas and the simple problems. It starts with everything being normal, then something occurs, the problem is solved and everything's normal again. You don't have to worry about missing an episode because nothing much happens. *The Brady Bunch* is very sexist compared with shows today. The boys were more important than the girls. The older you were the better you were. We feel we are more intelligent these days. Our problems today are more realistic and more difficult to solve. (Find the Feelings and What If ...? thinking tools will help you to compare and analyse.)

4. Add to: predict and invent

Television shows and soapies show similarities to *The Brady Bunch*. *Step By Step*, *Full House* and *Family Matters* are comparable. *The Brady Bunch* was influential and like a role model for people in the 1960s; perhaps many people felt they should be like the roles portrayed in the show. More realistic problems are tackled in today's shows such as *South Park* or *The Simpsons*. Are the characters in the shows viewed as role models today? Do these shows influence people to believe that some things are 'normal'? (Use the Pidgeonhole It and What If ...? thinking tools to develop some of the ideas from the shows.)

5. Judge: evaluate and rank

Was *The Brady Bunch* meant to influence a generation? Did it cause unhappiness because people did not conform to *The Brady Bunch* standards? The characters are 'goody-goody', stuck up, boring, fake. The child actors did it for the money. Did this make them happy? Has acting in the shows affected their lives? Shows copy each other. The show tries to be funny. *The Simpsons* is funny. In *The Brady Bunch* it takes them such a long time to solve a little problem. Older people like to watch it, perhaps to relive that simpler time. On the other hand *The Simpsons*, being a cartoon, at first glance appears to be more unreal, but because the issues brought up are real, the show seems more real than *The Brady Bunch*. (Use the Good, Bad and Curious thinking tool. This is Russian Salad thinking.)

The Five Good Thinking Steps
Russian Salad thinking

5. Judge
Evaluate and rank
(Good, Bad and Curious)

4. Add to
Predict and invent
(What If …?)

3. Compare
Examine and contrast
(What If …? Find the feelings)

2. Understand
Classify and define
(Pigeonhole It)

1. Explain
Show and identify
(Find the Facts)

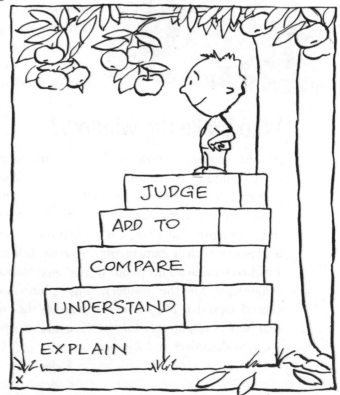

Bit of Biscuit thinking

When using the Good Thinking Steps, you don't have to use all of the steps for every discussion. Choose the steps you want to use depending on the topic. You can vary the order of the steps, except for step one – Explain – which is always the basis of a discussion.

When your children ask, 'What more can I do with my project?' remind them to check through the thinking tools of Find the Facts (knowledge), Pigeonhole It (classifying), asking What If ...? and Find the Feelings about the topic (analysing, comparing), to evaluate ideas using Good, Bad and Curious (reporting, illustrating, comparing, evaluating, debating and judging).

Remember that knowledge on its own is Bit of Biscuit thinking, but when knowledge is combined with thinking tools and strategies to make judgements about an idea, it becomes part of Russian Salad thinking.

Who broke the window?

Another analogy to show the difference between simple knowledge and more complex evaluation concerns the difference between simply jumping to conclusions by looking at a photo as proof and the complex process of gathering evidence and reasoning undertaken by a judge. Imagine that a house is broken into. A window is smashed, and a passerby with a camera photographs Bill in the garden near the smashed window. This photo is used as evidence to prove that Bill was responsible for the robbery. The photo can represent the fact (knowledge) that Bill was at the scene of the crime, but it is not proof that he was responsible for the robbery. To work out if he really was, we need detectives and a judge.

What do judges do? Judges listen carefully to all the evidence and proof that is put before them. They sift through the facts to find the most important and relevant ones, and they listen to both sides of the story.

In our example, the judge would learn that Bill just went to get his dog from the garden where it had run to get a ball. Several witnesses collaborated his story. Detectives would have reported that there was no evidence that Bill had been responsible for theft in the past, and no evidence that he had any of the stolen articles.  The fact that Bill had arthritis and was incapable of raising his legs to crawl through the window was further evidence. To make sense of what really happened the judge would have had to put a great deal of effort and thought into the matter. Only then could the judge come to an informed decision.

This is what we are going to do with Enhanced Thinking. We are going to try to be judges. We will learn to look further into the issue, and not just jump to conclusions on flimsy evidence. We are going to examine all the evidence and make informed decisions.

Enhanced Thinking

8

Experience is not what happens to you.
It is what you do with what happens to you.

Aldous Huxley 1894–1963

Think about someone you consider to be a good thinker. What are some of their qualities? Perhaps they're perceptive; they're observant and good listeners; they're confident and flexible in their thinking; they're creative and constructive; they can see all the issues; they make sense of things that have happened and learn from mistakes; they have original and pertinent points to add to the discussion; they see ramifications and consequences that others might have missed; they find different ways to look at and solve problems. Such a person is an Enhanced Thinker.

What is Enhanced Thinking?

* It is *creative* thinking (where you create new ideas in an inventive, imaginative way)
* It is *reflective* thinking (where you ask yourself questions to help you step through issues by finding out why you think as you do)
* It is *questioning* thinking (where you ask questions to help you find out how your concepts are linked to earlier or predicted or current ideas)

* It is *critical* thinking (where you examine, analyse and evaluate the concept)
* It is *insightful* thinking (where you have insight, and take into account other people's ideas, beliefs and values)

Big Important Concepts

Big Important Concepts are embedded in most of the issues that you discuss. These are the important, significant and weighty issues. Concepts such as truth and lies, good and bad, power both deliberate and accidental, needing and wanting, relationships, values, trust, cause and effect, human and animal rights, responsibility, ownership, justice, fairness, blame, perception, reality and nonreality, problems and mysteries, dreams and hopes, promises, winning and losing.

Look for and find these issues. When Enhanced Thinking is applied to Big Important Concepts the child becomes conscious of concepts that are essential to recognise and understand.

The aim of Enhanced Thinking

The aim of Enhanced Thinking is to encourage children to feel confident, empowered and aware of themselves and aware of issues, so they can thoughtfully find their priorities and make decisions.

Enhanced Thinking helps children:

* to understand themselves ('What do *I* think about the issue?' 'What is *my* experience of it?')
* to explore ideas and expand their thinking processes, making links, connections and comparisons with other ideas and concepts
* to understand the complexities of issues
* to make thoughtful decisions

Thinking strategies for Enhanced Thinking

Good or Enhanced Thinkers use a wide range of thinking strategies to help them think.

* Examining evidence, being aware of complexities and all the different issues that are relevant
* Researching, interpreting and analysing information
* Questioning, playing devil's advocate, debating and arguing
* Reflecting about the many and varied issues
* Making generalities, prioritising, inferring, justifying and identifying assumptions you have made
* Using similes, metaphors and analogies and stories to help explain so the concepts can be understood

An analogy – learning to drive

Let's think for a moment about driving a car. Every day you get in a car and 'just drive'. If you have driven for some time, chances are that the activity is very much 'automatic'. Some reflective thinking can help us to find some of the things that back up your 'automatic' driving.

When we were first married, Ted and I lived in a mining town in the country. We were the proud owners of a Land Rover with a big cabin constructed on the back, a bit like a mini-caravan. I hadn't learnt to drive and I was desperate to be able to do so. My desire for the freedom to be able to drive myself to school, to visit friends and go to the shops motivated me. I was aware of the benefits of driving and certainly aware of the dangers and responsibility of driving.

Ted agreed to give me driving lessons. Can you remember your first driving lesson and how impossibly complicated the whole process appeared to be? Learning to drive in a vehicle with a built-in caravan was no easy matter, but bit by bit, I learnt how to do it.

First I learnt how to use the gears and then, with much lurching and jolting, I learnt to coordinate the gear changes with the clutch. I familiarised myself with the accelerator and the brake and progressed from driving in a car park to actually taking the Land Rover on the road. At the same time, I learnt all the road rules, at first as bits of information then gradually with further understanding of their values, as I put them into practice.

I learnt about roads; how to drive on rough bush tracks, how to avoid potholes and corrugations, and how to be careful when moving onto the dirt edge of a sealed road. I also learnt to drive in town.

Think of driving a car as a series of circles like a bull's-eye target:

* Your approach. First of all, and most importantly, there is your approach, your attitudes and how you go about it.
* Keys. Second are the keys you use, and how you actually drive the car. This includes knowing about the workings of your car and the road rules.
* Tools. Third is your experience and knowledge of what to do in certain circumstances. You know to take things more slowly when it's wet, to take care when driving at night, to dim your lights when approaching another car.

Enhanced Thinking in a bull's-eye

We can adapt the bull's-eye analogy to explain Enhanced Thinking.

* Approach. The attitude and understanding of thinking aloud, encouragement, creative and reflective thinking, using similes and analogies, and understanding of Big Important Concepts such as truth and fairness. Both children and adults need to approach Enhanced Thinking in a positive, interested way.
* Keys. Adults introduce stories or objects which will interest their children. Children use the keys, which can be stories or objects, to unlock their thoughts about an idea or issue.
* Thinking tools. Adults show and demonstrate thinking tools to their children who use a variety of thinking tools – such as Good, Bad and Curious, and Find the Facts to open up and focus on issues and ideas.

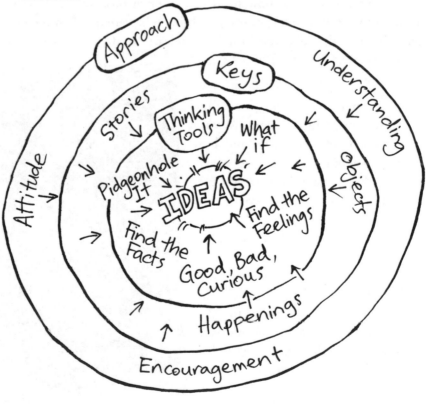

Enhanced
Thinking in action

Thinking is the hardest work there is. That's why so few people do it.
Henry Ford 1863–1947

A newspaper article can be used to illustrate Enhanced Thinking in action. I use the article like a key to open up the minds of a group of children. I use, and you can use, thinking tools to tackle lots of issues embedded in the article.

On their own, these issues would be difficult to broach with children without seeming a bit heavy or contrived. As part of the newspaper article, children can pull out the issues themselves, given a little nudge in the right direction. They will be very pleased with themselves for thinking about so many issues.

'Eggstraordinary' egg

'Metal spade nearly foils fortune hunt.' Three children were digging in the sand on a West Australian beach when they came across a large, hard, egg-shaped object. They reburied it, returned home and investigated what it was by reading books and asking at a museum. The children discovered that it was an elephant bird egg from Madagascar. A collector heard that they had found the egg and offered them money for it; the West Australian Government set up an appeal to raise money to purchase the egg so that it could be displayed in a museum.

Eventually, when the children and their parents returned to the deserted coastline and they located the cross they had made on the sand with branches, their spade hit the egg. Luckily no damage was done! (See the photo below.) The children got the money and the museum got the egg.

Use some thinking tools to open up the issues: Pigeonhole It, Find the Facts, Find the Feelings, and Good, Bad and Curious.

Pigeonhole It

This exercise will help your children to find out about team playing and rules. Pretend that you are the children who found the egg and work out some rules that will help you work as a team of 'Egg Keepers'. You and your children can work out

some of the rules to be a good team player in any group or team. These might include:

* Listen
* Have mutual respect
* Treat everyone equally
* You would need to decide if it would be better to give team members roles like a manager or a treasurer (examine the good and bad points of doing things formally)
* Give everyone a go
* Treat everyone as you would wish to be treated
* Don't put people down
* Don't say mean things
* Don't brag
* Don't boss
* Don't get jealous
* Don't spread rumours
* Don't gang up on one person

Reasons and excuses

What is the difference between a reason and an excuse?

Use this story to explore the differences between reasons and excuses. Find some examples of reasons and excuses? Discuss whether what you regard as a reason other people might regard as an excuse. Make your own definitions for 'reason' and 'excuse'. This topic might set off quite a heated discussion, but next time the issue comes up you'll have a reference point to argue from.

Eggs

Classify eggs and Pigeonhole Them in order of size, their colour, if you can eat them or not, name all the creatures that lay eggs. How many birds can you name? Have a competition to see who can name the most egg-laying creatures. The prize could be a jelly snake (snakes lay eggs).

Museum

The elephant bird egg ended up in a museum. Discuss and classify what a museum is. Find organisations that are similar to museums: art galleries, aquariums, exhibitions, art shows. Is an art gallery the same as a museum? In some parts of the world, art galleries are called museums. How are they similar? How are they different? Perhaps you could have a discussion about museums and discuss open questions such as:

* What is a museum for?
* What should museums contain?
* Why are things from the past important?
* How are things looked after in a museum?
* Would it be interesting or boring to work in a museum?
* What is work?
* What makes things boring?
* Is work boring?
* What makes work boring?

How did the egg get there?

Look for Madagascar on a map. Use your imagination to come up with a reason why the egg ended up on the West Australian coast. Classify ways the egg could have travelled across the ocean:

* A bird was carried across (by winds or on a ship) and laid the egg
* The egg was washed across the ocean by the tides
* A sailor was shipwrecked and buried his precious good luck egg
* Pirates buried it
* There are lots of eggs in the dunes because a long time ago elephant birds used it as a breeding ground

Find the Facts

It's really helpful to be able to find the facts in issues or discussions. Use this thinking tool to summarise the facts from the article. For example, 'Three children found a mysterious egg, they reburied it and investigated it ...'

You may find it easier to use this thinking tool in the discussion by pointing out the difference between opinions and facts. List the facts in order of importance, find other examples that would fit Find the Facts.

Your children might enjoy discussing a newspaper article and finding the facts. Every time someone mentions an opinion rather than a fact they have to pick up a toothpick. At the end, the person with the least number of toothpicks wins.

Show your children you are interested in their game, make funny comments, add your own ideas. Give the winner a pat on the back and some words of praise for having such a sharp mind. Make sure you comment on a brilliant idea the other players came up with and praise their efforts, too.

Find the Feelings

To get in touch with emotions we could ask ourselves how would *we* feel if *we* were the children, their parents, the collector or the government? What would make us feel excited, angry, cheated, frustrated, proud, clever or lucky? Role play with your children, taking turns at being the parents, the children, the person in the government and the collector.

Good, Bad and Curious

The elephant bird egg provides a great opportunity to put the Good, Bad and Curious thinking tool into practice. Discuss finding the egg.

Good

- ☑ Exciting
- ☑ Famous
- ☑ Story would be in the newspapers and on television
- ☑ People could see what an elephant bird egg looked like
- ☑ Scientists could study it
- ☑ Reward money for the children
- ☑ More visitors for the museum

Bad

- ☒ Jealousy and difficulty dividing the money
- ☒ Who actually found the egg?
- ☒ Should they have an equal share of the money?

Curious

Look for the 'invisible issues' such as jealousy, competition and right and wrong.

- ❓ Who owns the egg?
- ❓ What is the difference between payment and reward?
- ❓ What is a reward?
- ❓ Is finders keepers?
- ❓ Does the monetary value of a thing determine if you can keep it if you find it?
- ❓ What about sentimental and historical value?
- ❓ If it's decided that we can keep five cents if we find it, would the same rule apply in a country where five cents is a lot of money?
- ❓ Why do we have money?
- ❓ Who invented money?
- ❓ What is a bribe?
- ❓ What is stealing?
- ❓ Who owns what is in the ground?
- ❓ The law states that because the egg was found on Crown Land the children had no right to the egg. Is this fair?
- ❓ Would it be different if the children found the egg in their own backyard?
- ❓ Would the issue of money for the egg be different if an adult had found the egg?

? Do we treat children and adults differently?

? Do we show more support and encouragement because they are children?

? Were the children clever to find the egg?

? How do we know it is really an elephant bird egg?

? Can the egg help scientists?

? How do we know it's a real egg and not a fake?

? Would we have buried the egg if we had found it?

? Would it have been better if they had not found the egg?

? What if they had damaged the egg with the spade?

Big Important Concepts

From the Good, Bad and Curious points we can discover the Big Important Concepts embedded in the elephant bird egg story.

Ownership

Who owns the egg?

* The children?
* The Australian government?
* The Madagascan government?
* The elephant bird?
* All Australians?
* Is reward and payment to do with ownership?
* What does it mean to own something?
* What do we own?
* How do we know we own it?
* Do we own our stories and ideas?

Real or unreal?

* Is an elephant bird a real or imaginary bird?
* How do we know the difference between reality and unreality?
* Does what we believe affect what we see; or does what we see affect what we believe?
* Did someone dream up the whole story?
* What is the difference between a dream and a daydream?
* What is wishful thinking?
* Is it the same as pretending?

* Is pretending a lie?
* What is a lie?
* What about the things that seem real but are not real?
* What about the things that seem false but are real?

How do we know things? Who should we believe?

* How did the children know it was an elephant bird egg?
* How did the children find out what it was?
* Would a person from a museum study and investigate the egg?
* Would a university be another place to try?
* What proof would you need to believe what you are told?
* Should we believe everything adults tell us?

Good, Bad and Curious

Use the Good, Bad and Curious thinking tool to discuss adults and what they may or may not say to children. Should children believe everything adults say?

Good

✓ They know things
✓ They may be wiser as they may have learnt from their mistakes
✓ They might know the truth
✓ They can be reassuring

Bad

✗ Sometimes they try to trick children
✗ Sometimes when they trick children bad adults might have harmful things in mind
✗ They sometimes exaggerate (So that the kids get the message? To make kids feel guilty? So kids won't do it again?)
✗ They might guess the wrong thing
✗ They may be being sarcastic
✗ They may not know what is true

Curious

? Do adults sometimes talk about things they don't really know about?
? Do adults sometimes say something because they think it's the appropriate thing to say?
? Is is sometimes simpler not to question adults?
? Do children sometimes pretend to believe adults when they don't really believe them?
? What's the difference between lying, and exaggerating, and being sarcastic and joking?
? Do adults believe some things because of their taste?
? What is taste?

What is stealing?

✳ Is all stealing bad? If something valuable or rare is stolen is that worse? Are there degrees of stealing?
✳ What is borrowing or lending? How are they different from or similar to stealing?

* If we steal something from someone then someone steals it from us is this as bad?
* If we accidentally take something is this as bad?
* What part of stealing is worse – the intention or having possession of something that is not yours?
* Is it different if you steal something and feel guilty, or if you don't care?

What If ...?

What if you were there when the three children found the egg? Make up some arguments they could have had:

* 'It's mine ... I found it!'
* 'But it was my idea to dig for treasure.'
* 'But you're all staying at my house ... you would never even be here if it was not for me!'
* 'I want to sell it to get lots of money.'
* 'I want to keep it to hand down to my kids.'
* 'What if someone steals the egg?'
* 'What if the house burns down?'

From these examples, you can see that wonderful discussions can grow out of a simple newspaper article. The important part of your conversation is the ideas – the Big Important Concepts.

Initially you might need to practise and concentrate on finding and using the thinking tool that is right for the specific discussion, but soon you will find that selecting the right tool becomes automatic (just as you automatically select the bread knife to cut the bread and the small paring knife to slice a carrot). The thinking tools are useful to help you to open up issues and ideas. Become familiar and comfortable with using the tools, then concentrate on the wonderful ideas your children will produce.

Pigeonhole It

I do love cricket — it's so very English.

Sarah Bernhardt 1844–1923 (on seeing a game of football)

In the previous chapter the elephant bird egg article gives an example of classifying or organising objects or ideas into groups. This provides an ideal opportunity to chase ideas with children. This section explores and develops the importance of classifying or pigeonholing information and ideas.

The Pigeonhole It game

When you're chasing ideas, play the Pigeonhole It game to classify things. Explain to your children that the word 'pigeonhole' comes from holes in a wall for pigeons to nest in, and that the word has come to mean 'filing things'.

You can adapt this game to the age and interests of your children. Pigeonhole It is fun. From the time they can talk, children are constantly trying to see where things fit, to sort, to find relationships, to discover similarities and differences between objects and people.

You can start by getting younger children to sort items into different categories. Get them to place all the spoons together and the forks together; or help unpack the shopping bags, separating condiments, biscuits, cooking ingredients, fresh fruit, fresh vegetables;

or make piles of their favourite toys. Organising chess pieces or playing cards according to colour or type can be an engrossing task for young children. Children need to assess and judge and make decisions to sort objects, they need to use Enhanced Thinking.

Older children are constantly hard at work classifying other ideas, like: What is a friend? What is fair? What do I need? The Pigeonhole It game can be adapted to any age group, depending on the subject or topic chosen.

Be enthusiastic about your children's mental gymnastics. As icing on the cake you can make an incorrect statement about a category and let your children kindly explain where you have gone wrong!

This playing with ideas can be revisited when relevant points surface again in later months or years. Record your ideas in your Thinking Trap Resource Book. Just a few minutes recording these ideas will:

* reinforce your interest in your children's ideas
* provide a record to refer back to, add to, or fine tune
* help 'capture' the discussion so that all the wonderful ideas don't vanish into thin air

Everyday things for the Pigeonhole It game

Here are some questions to wonder about, and some points to evaluate, with your children. Included are some ideas to start off your thinking. You'll quickly find your own ideas and topics to play the Pigeonhole It game. Have lots of fun; try to outdo each other to find different, original, wild and unusual ideas.

For very young children you can play the Pigeonhole It game in dozens of ways. Simply place a wide selection of objects (toothbrush, earring, almond, band-aid, ring, teaspoon, orange, hazelnut, shampoo and so forth) on a table. Next ask the children to group the objects in as many ways as they can think. For example they might group them by their use, their shape, their colour, the material they

are made from, edible objects, size (large objects, small objects), by colour grading (light coloured to dark coloured) or any other way you can find. As your children change the objects in a group, they explain why the object fits the new group.

When you play the Pigeonhole It game, timing is important. Use something you have seen or heard as an introduction to think up some objects or ideas to classify. For example after you've seen a child do something smart, comment on how clever kids are. Ask your children the following:

What can children do better than adults?

Discuss ways to classify the characteristics of children.

* Climb trees
* Run
* Get into small places
* Grow
* Copy
* Use their imagination
* Eat sweets
* Know more hiding places in the house
* Play with toys
* Learn
* Hang upside down on the monkey bars
* Draw
* Be scared of the bogeyman (This is interesting. Is the word 'better' the right word to use for something that may *not* be good? – see the following points)
* Make mistakes
* Make a mess
* Break things
* Whine

What can adults do better than children?

Judge and classify what it is to be an adult.

* Look after kids
* Look after the house

* Look after clothes
* Look after themselves
* Look after people
* Earn money
* Know what money's worth
* Spend money
* Budget
* Drive
* Cook
* Know when enough is enough
* Think of consequences
* Keep tidy
* Aware of danger
* Boss
* Keep secrets
* Resist things

Why do people swear?

If you have heard someone swear, you can wonder about swearing and why people swear.

* Because of stress and frustration
* Because they are mad at someone or something
* Because things are wrong and out of control
* Because they have the habit of swearing
* To joke
* To impress
* To shock
* To seem cool

Truth and lies: why do people tell fibs?

If someone you know has been caught out telling a lie, this provides a perfect time for you and your children to explore issues of truth and lies and white lies. Why do people lie?

* To avoid trouble
* To make others jealous
* To impress people

* To be liked by friends
* To be popular
* To get attention
* So as not to hurt someone's feelings (white lies)
* To make people feel better (white lies)
* Because they're embarrassed
* Because they're jealous
* For a joke
* To trick people

Reasons and excuses

Continue your discussion about the elephant bird egg. Look for examples of reasons and excuses. What is the difference between an excuse and a reason?

* Is a reason the same as an excuse?
* Is an excuse the same as a reason?
* Is an excuse more about not wanting to be blamed?
* Might a reason have more truth than an excuse?

Truth and lies

If you are talking about a fib, a fake or a forgery, wonder about the 'grey' area, degrees of truth, or the reasons for copying. Your children will be puzzled about things that are not 'black' or 'white'. It is interesting to try to find differences in the degree of truth or making things up or twisting the truth. Can there be degrees of truth? Now this is a hard question to think about!

 ## Find the Feelings about being told the truth or a fib

Discuss how you have felt when you told a fib or when someone told you a fib.

Some Curious points about the truth

* What's the difference between something that is true, a lie, a fake, a forgery and a hoax? (Truth: that which is true, a verified or indisputable fact. Lie: telling something that is not the truth. Hoax: tricks or mischievous jokes. Fake: imitation, acting, false nails, eyelashes, ads. Forgery: money, signature, illegal copying.)

* Is fiction made up of nonfiction?
* Can we tell a crook by the way they look?
* What about half-truths? Silence? Leaving bits out?
* What about exaggerating?
* How do we know what is true?
* If you make people jump to conclusions without telling a lie, is this still lying?
* Is 'truth' different things to different people?
* Should you tell a lie to help someone feel better? (If a child has broken her arm, should you delay telling her the truth until she is at the hospital, and the arm can be taken care of?)
* What is a white lie? (An unimportant lie? A lie to make someone feel better?)
* What is a big lie?
* Is stretching the truth lying?
* Is the more the truth is stretched the bigger the lie, or the more believable the lie, the worse it is?
* If sometimes we don't want to know the truth, and someone tells us what we want to hear instead, is that a lie?
* Why don't we like being lied to?
* Is it always fair to tell the truth?

Where do ideas and thoughts come from?

When someone has a great idea or makes a brilliant suggestion, wonder about where ideas come from. Ask your child 'Where did you get that good idea from?' and compile a list in your Thinking Trap Resource Book or on a piece of paper stuck to the fridge. Your list will show different ways people get ideas. It will be fun to watch the list grow. Your children's awareness of how they can get an idea if they are stuck for inspiration will be growing with this list.

You can get ideas from:

* Reading something
* Hearing something
* Speaking – you hear the words and suddenly you realise they make sense, and you have solved the problem
* From the back of your mind
* From memories

Ralph had tried so hard to protect himself from new ideas, only to find out that they came from within.

* Things being triggered by other things
* By looking and watching
* From television, books, films and the Internet
* Pictures and photographs

What is a hero?

If your child admires a sports star, a pop star appears on television, or there is a news item about a hero, use the opportunity to discuss heroes. Find characteristics heroes have in common:

* People who risk their lives to save people
* Someone who has sacrificed for others

* A survivor
* Famous singers, actors and so forth
* Sports people
* Santa
* Superman

When you see someone do something really brave, or if there is a news report about bravery, or if your child has been brave use this as an opportunity to discuss bravery.

What is a mask?

When your child wears a mask to a party or to play a game, use the mask to wonder about masks:

* A mask is something you put on your face to look different
* Can an expression be a mask?
* Is make-up a mask?
* Is plastic surgery a mask?
* It can be for protection (fencing mask)
* Is blushing a mask?

Animals for the Pigeonhole It game

You can have a lot of fun trying to find as many different ways as you can of classifying animals using the Pigeonhole It game. When you start this thinking game you might all like to guess how many classifications you will find. You will be amazed at the new ideas that will be squeezed out of your children's heads as they try to reach the number they predicted.

In his book *The Order of Things: An Archaeology of the Human Sciences*, Michel Foucault quotes an ancient Chinese encyclopedia that divided animals into '(a) belonging to the Emperor (b) embalmed (c) tame (d) sucking pigs (e) sirens (f) fabulous (g) stray dogs (h) included in the present classification (i) frenzied (j) innumerable (k) drawn with a fine camel hair brush (l) et cetera (m) having just broken the water pitcher (n) that from a very long way off look like flies.'

You can discuss this quote and put all the animals into 'made-up' classifications. You may then like to try putting the animals into another category. The creativity of your categories and the animals you select will depend on the age of your children. A running commentary might look a bit like this:

A to Z: Anteater, armadillo, ant, butterfly, baboon, bat, bear, cub, crab, crocodile, crayfish, camel, cat, caterpillar, dog, dingo, dragon, dolphin, donkey, elephant, eel, flounder, fox, fly, gorilla, guinea pig, griffin, goat, gibbon, horse, hippo, iguana, joey, kangaroo, koala, lion, lizard, leopard, lobster, mouse, monkey, numbat, octopus, platypus, possum, porcupine, quokka, rabbit, rat, rhinoceros, shark, seal, snake, snow leopard, tiger, tropical fish, unicorn, viper, vulture, vicuña, wart hog, whale, wolf, yak, zebra

Small animals: (How do you define small?) platypus (also fits into the category of animals with beaks and animals with claws, water animal, fantastic animals, mammals and Australian animals), rabbit (also pet, wild animal and pest), lizard, (also reptile), guinea pig (also tail-less animals, pet animal, animals that can be eaten), cat, snake, koala, possum, eel, fox, dingo, flounder, tortoise, butterfly, ant

Fabulous or mythical animals: dragon, unicorn, griffin, Loch Ness Monster, Humphrey B. Bear, Big Ted, Big Bird, Oscar, ET, Mickey Mouse, Blinky Bill, Troll, Ewok, Daffy, Daisy, Minnie, Goofy, Pluto

Camouflaged animals: flounder, grasshopper, chameleon, stick insect, stick spider, moth, bug, leopard

Endangered animals: elephant, rhinoceros, numbat, prairie dog, toucan, dugong, hairy-nosed wombat, bilby, ghost bat, hump-backed whale

Dangerous animals: shark, snake, frog, spider, crown-of-thorns starfish, scorpion, stonefish, puffer fish, blue-ringed octopus, Portuguese man-o'-war, crocodile

Animals people eat: chicken, pig, frog (legs), cow, cattle, goat, snake, kangaroo, crocodile, sheep, duck, bug, fish and eggs, shark fin, turtle, horns of rhino, emu eggs, dog, fish, lobster, octopus, squid, prawn, scallop, oyster, clam

Animals that eat people: vulture, shark, piranha, crab

Animals with jaws: lion, crocodile, dog, dingo, cats, bear, shark, monkey, fish

Carnivorous animals: vulture, dog, cat, snake, shark, tiger, lion, jaguar, bear, dinosaur

Animals with claws: bear, cat, dog, crocodile, bird, lion, rabbit, guinea pig, dingo, monkey

Animals with paws: bear, car, dog, lion, monkey

Big cats: lion, cheetah, leopard, tiger

Animals from hot places: monkey, elephant, giraffe, gibbon, armadillo, tropical fish, hippopotamus, camel

House and farm animals: horse, donkey, dog, cat, sheep, goat

Wild bush animals: bear, kangaroo, anteater, wart hog, wolf, dingo

Sea or water animals: octopus, seal, dolphin, whale, shark, flounder, platypus

Pests: mosquito, rabbit, fly, carp fish, crown-of-thorns starfish

Extinct animals: dinosaur, Tasmanian tiger, dodo

Animals that lay eggs: platypus, turtle, bird, frog, ant, emu, butterfly, fish, snake

Fast animals: platypus, crocodile, fox, dingo, cheetah

Animals with a shell or armour: snail, crab, prawn, turtle, tortoise

Animals that go crazy: lemming, animal with rabies, hyena

Nocturnal animals, insects, animals that live on land, sea or air – the list is endless.

Play Good, Bad and Curious

I think, at a child's birth, if a mother could ask a fairy godmother to endow it with the most useful gift, that gift would be curiosity.

Eleanor Roosevelt 1884–1962

The Good, Bad and Curious thinking tool can be particularly useful in validating and emphasising the importance of curiosity. The tool gives children strategies to help them judge events, actions and rights (both their own rights and the rights of other people). Chase ideas and identify different opinions and interpretations, discover and solve problems and judge if things are right or wrong.

Objects can be powerful keys to open children's minds. Children have a fascination with the notion that discussions can come out of objects. It's like a form of magic to them. I have had wonderful fun and astonishing discussions with children simply by using an object as a key.

Using everyday objects

Everyday objects can be used as keys to unlock children's thoughts. By discussing issues raised by considering the object, children can discover ideas about fairness, rules, laws, rights and needs for themselves. Find objects that can be used as symbols, objects that represent ideas, objects that tell about the past, and objects that have an interesting story attached to them.

Magic wands

If you see a magic wand in a shop, or if your children have a magic wand, play a make-believe game and pretend that magic wands are real. Watch their eyes sparkle as they pretend they could have anything they wanted! What if magic wands were real? These are some of the ideas that might come up:

Good

- ✓ You could live forever
- ✓ You could cast spells
- ✓ You could be anything you want
- ✓ You could have anything
- ✓ You could do anything
- ✓ You could help sick people
- ✓ You could bring the dead back to life
- ✓ You could do tricks
- ✓ You could make people disappear
- ✓ The world could be free of hunger, sickness, wars and death
- ✓ You would have enormous power
- ✓ You could have a new house
- ✓ You could win the lottery
- ✓ You could have a lion for a pet
- ✓ You could turn back time
- ✓ You could fly
- ✓ You could stay well
- ✓ You could stay slim in spite of eating the wrong food

Bad

- ✗ It would be confusing if people turned you into a frog
- ✗ What if you couldn't correct mistakes made by using magic?
- ✗ People could be turned into ugly things, and have curses put on them
- ✗ Crimes could be committed without leaving a clue

Curious

- ? Whose wand would have the most power?
- ? Would the 'good' people's wand have the most power?
- ? What if you pretended to be good just to get power?

? How would we judge people to find the 'good' people?
? Would wands make you lazy?
? What if you lost your wand?
? Would wands make you more selfish?
? Would you just want more and more?
? Would children need to go to wand school to learn rules of how to use a wand?
? Would there need to be rules on how to use a wand safely and fairly?
? Would people be happier if they could have anything they want?
? Is the hoping and planning as good as the getting?
? Would people be bored if they didn't need to work?

Things we wouldn't need if we all had a magic wand

* Schools
* Universities (we could wish to know everything)
* Shops (but how would we know what to wish for if we couldn't see things in shops? Do people enjoy shopping for other reasons?)
* Hospitals
* Doctors
* Nurses
* Old people's homes
* Dentists
* Undertakers
* Competitive things: sports, the Olympic Games, chess, card games, board games
* Work

What if you could make three wishes for the world?

* People would stop littering and polluting
* Fighting and wars would stop
* There would be no more robbers
* People would not hurt or kill animals
* Driftnets would no longer be used
* All illness and disease could be cured

What if you could make three wishes for your life?

* To be happy
* To have a good job

Darling, you wouldn't happen to know anything about why my clothes have suddenly changed into gingerbread, would you?

* To be happily married
* To have a happy healthy family
* To have money
* To be a millionaire
* To have contentment
* To have wisdom
* To have a long life
* To keep your friends
* To make your family happy
* To reach your potential

Bike helmets

A bike helmet can be used as a key to think imaginatively about issues such as rules, laws and changes, and to solve problems and to look for consequences. Play with ideas. Ask your children: what if a law were passed saying everyone has to wear a helmet all the time?

Good

- ☑ The helmet would protect heads
- ☑ There would be less head injury
- ☑ Toddlers could fall over and not hurt their heads
- ☑ Shops that sold helmets would get lots of money

Bad

- ☒ Hair would be knotted and hard to keep tidy
- ☒ It would be hard to wash and dry hair
- ☒ It would be hard to swim
- ☒ People may drown
- ☒ People would get headaches and be grumpy
- ☒ It would be difficult to sleep
- ☒ It would hurt babies
- ☒ Toddlers would overbalance and fall over

Curious

- ❓ What does 'all of the time' mean?
- ❓ What about when your head grew too big for the helmet?
- ❓ Would there be special helmets for weddings or school and so forth?
- ❓ Would we get used to wearing helmets?
- ❓ How would poor people be able to afford to buy a helmet?
- ❓ What if you didn't want to wear a helmet?
- ❓ How would you be punished for breaking the law?
- ❓ Would helmets be made fashionable?
- ❓ What is fashion?
- ❓ Is fashion good or bad?
- ❓ Clothes would need to be designed with big necks
- ❓ Coffins would need to be bigger

Shampoo

A bottle of shampoo can be used as a key to open up discussions about the rights of animals and scientific testing and the rights of people. The information you share with your children depends on their age and how they will cope with the knowledge.

- ✳ Why do shampoos get tested on animals?
- ✳ Is it fair to use animals for experimentation?

* Should products be tested on people?
* How should people treat animals?
* How should people treat people?
* Should people have the right to do what they want?
* Is it fair if you do something you want to do but it hurts someone else?

Eggs

Another way to open up a discussion about animals and animal rights is an egg. Battery farming of poultry can be discussed and compared with barn-laid and farmyard eggs for this discussion. The last four questions from the shampoo 'key' can be discussed.

Beans

A green bean or a can of baked beans can be used as a key. As you open a can of baked beans, or prepare green beans, ask your children, 'What story has beans in it?' The answer is of course the story *Jack and the Beanstalk*. Wonder about Jack. Was he good or bad?

Good

Perhaps you will discover that Jack was good because he tried to help his mother, he gave the gold to his mum, he was brave, he used his initiative, he was inquisitive.

Bad

Jack was bad because he was disobedient, he didn't sell the cow for money, he was gullible (he believed the crazy tale of the bean seller), he was a thief (he stole the giant's goose, though in some versions of the story the goose originally belonged to Jack's family so he was just taking back what was rightfully his), he was a murderer (he killed the giant).

Curious

? Is it ever right to disobey?
? Can curiosity be wrong?
? Is it wrong to be gullible?
? What is luck?
? Did they live happily ever after?
? Did Jack feel guilty because he killed the giant?

? Is stealing always wrong?

? Is stealing for a good cause okay?

? Did the giant deserve to be killed?

? Is it okay to kill someone to save lives?

? If you're poor do you take more chances as you have nothing to lose?

? Are adults always right?

? Why did Jack believe the man who gave him the beans?

The sun

A perfect sunny day, too much sun and sunburn, or a picnic ruined by rain and no sun, can provide the opportunity to start up a discussion about the sun.

Good

✓ Without sunlight plants couldn't grow and nothing could live on earth

✓ Holidays are better with sunshine

✓ We're happy when the sun is out

✓ We need it for warmth

✓ Light comes from the sun

✓ Good for solar panels

✓ It feels good in summer to tan and only wear a few clothes

Bad

✗ Skin cancer

✗ Sunburn

✗ Burning your feet on the hot sand at the beach

✗ Drought

✗ Dries up the garden

✗ Bush fires

✗ Feel faint or sick when it is too hot

Curious

? Why did some people worship the sun?

? Are we dependent on the sun for life?

? How do people manage in countries such as Iceland, when they have darkness with no sun during the day in the winter?

? What would it be like to live in a country where during summer there was no night – to have sunshine at midnight?

The wind

On a windy day, use the wind as a key to open a discussion of the fable about the competition between the sun and the wind. They had been arguing about who was more powerful when they noticed a man walking down a road. They decided to have a competition to see who could make the man take off his coat. Firstly it was the wind's turn. The harder it blew, the tighter the man wrapped his overcoat around him. Then it was the sun's turn. The sun beamed down and the man took off his coat. This fable asks and answers the question of whether punishment or praise is best to make someone do something.

Look at the Good, Bad and Curious points about praise. Look at the Good, Bad and Curious points about punishment. Discuss what makes you do things. Is fear of punishment more powerful than praise? What is power? Who has power? Is it good to be in the power of someone? How do we become empowered? What does our self-talk tell us about power?

Crime and punishment

Select a time when the topic of punishment has come up in a newspaper article. Discuss punishment in general. At a later time, if your children are distressed about punishment of themselves or others you have established a framework to revisit and add to.

Good

✓ Teaches you not to make the same mistake twice, not to be careless or thoughtless or unkind
✓ Hurt person may feel better to see the person who hurt them punished

Bad

✗ Sometimes an innocent person gets punished
✗ If some people are punished they might want revenge
✗ Punishment can cause more trouble
✗ Some punishment may hurt a person for life

Curious

⸮ The type of punishment depends on what you've done
⸮ The punishment should fit the crime
⸮ Some people get let off punishment
⸮ What is fair punishment for a murderer?
⸮ Is there a difference if you do things accidentally or deliberately?
⸮ Sometimes punishment is not fair
⸮ Some people love getting attention when they are smacked
⸮ If you don't care what the punishment is, is it still punishment?

Fame

When you are discussing heroes or if you see someone famous (a film star, a world leader or famous sports person) on television or in a press article, use this opportunity to wonder about fame. Pretend you are famous.

Good

✓ Fans
✓ You're on television
✓ Media
✓ Everyone knows you
✓ Lots of attention
✓ Popular
✓ Cool
✓ Money
✓ Luxury
✓ Lots of friends
✓ Interesting friends
✓ People make an effort to be nice to you
✓ Feel important
✓ Special treatment
✓ Power

Bad

☒ No time to yourself
☒ Criticism
☒ Lack of privacy
☒ People might take photos of you when you don't want them to
☒ May be forced to do what you don't want to do
☒ Having to wear disguises to be free of attention
☒ Not in control
☒ May become too proud and think you're far too important
☒ May get kidnapped
☒ No safety
☒ Bodyguards
☒ Friends may use you
☒ Back-stabbing
☒ Fame fades

Curious

☒ Can money and fame buy happiness?
☒ Is fame an accident?
☒ Once you're famous you can't escape being famous
☒ Does fame mean power?

Think of some advice for someone who is going to be famous. For example:

✳ Don't show off
✳ Find your true friends
✳ Don't think you're the best
✳ Be yourself
✳ Use your money for good things
✳ Don't be too upset when you're no longer the centre of attention
✳ Don't diet too much
✳ Beware because the media will find out everything about you – you can't have secrets
✳ Fame doesn't last
✳ There will be rumors about you
✳ Beware of getting cheated
✳ Don't go overboard

* Beware of facelifts
* Not everyone will like you

You could talk about infamous people, such as criminals who are well known because of bad deeds they have done.

The Good, Bad and Curious thinking tool can open up many issues. As you can see, many Big Important Concepts come out of the discussions. What fun it is to observe children discovering some of these issues for themselves.

Don't forget to sum up after a thinking aloud discussion. For instance, if you have been talking about baked beans and Jack and good and bad, say with a hint of wonder in your voice, 'Isn't it amazing all these ideas have come out of a can of baked beans!' And you know of course they have. If you hadn't used the baked bean tin as a key, all the ideas you have just been discussing would still be locked away in your children's heads. Such magic from everyday things!

12

What's in our daily bread

A good laugh is sunshine in a house.

William Makepeace Thackeray 1811–1863

Chasing ideas can develop from a humble slice of bread and result in a whole range of complex discussions. Thinking, wondering, listening, speaking, reasoning, finding and developing links and further developing one's own philosophy of life can follow from ideas generated by thinking about simple everyday things.

We can use the Good, Bad and Curious, Find the Facts and Find the Feelings thinking tools to open up and expand ideas brought to mind by the bread.

The slice of bread is a key to focus our attention, and capture our curiosity, interest and imagination. The bread opens up awareness, connections, and conjures up past experience, knowledge and thoughts.

Good, Bad and Curious

To start this discussion it's important to have some warm, fresh bread. Give a slice of this warm bread to your children and say, 'I wonder if there could be a bread-led improvement in the economy of our state or country?'

Bread and rules

What if the government made a rule to say 'Everyone has to eat a slice of fresh bread every day'?

Good

- ☑ Demand for bread would increase
- ☑ Bread is good for your health compared to some things people eat
- ☑ More jobs generated
- ☑ More money for bread manufacturers, shops, wheat growers, truck drivers, plastic-bag makers
- ☑ More money for butter, jam, peanut-butter manufacturers
- ☑ It would be good for the homeless if the government paid for the bread

Bad

- ☒ It could lead to an unbalanced diet if people ate too much bread
- ☒ What if bread makes you sick?
- ☒ What if you were on a diet?
- ☒ What if you don't like bread?
- ☒ Would there be waste?
- ☒ Would bread be cheaper because if you manufacture a lot of an item the costs often go down?
- ☒ Would bread be more expensive as the manufacturers know you have to have bread daily no matter what it costs?
- ☒ Would it be hard for some people to get to the shops?
- ☒ Would people eat less of other foods?
- ☒ Would people get sick of bread?
- ☒ Would people protest?

Curious

- ? Who would pay for the bread?
- ? If the government pays for the bread, money would be wasted because most people can afford to buy bread
- ? If the government pays for the bread would the government make taxes go up to cover the cost?
- ? Where would the extra money come from?
- ? Would we be able to buy just one slice of bread? At schools and stations and shops?

? What does 'fresh' mean?

? What is a slice?

? What is bread? Is it the ingredients or how they are cooked? Scones? Toast? Pizza base?

? What is the difference between bread and cake? (Is it true that all bread can be buttered but not all cakes? Glue can be flour and water but it is not bread!)

? What if you could not eat yeast or were to have a medical operation requiring an empty stomach?

? Are there always exceptions to rules?

? Should we obey rules?

? How would it be known we had not obeyed the rule?

? If you break rules and get punished is that to teach you a lesson?

? What could be the punishment? (If the punishment were being forced to eat a whole loaf at the police station the starving would refuse to eat a slice so they would have a whole loaf!)

? What is fair punishment?

? Would people cheat?

? What is 'cheating'?

? What does 'eat' mean? If something is greasy and slips down without chewing is that eating?

? How would they know whether you had eaten fresh bread or not?

? What would you do with the leftover bread?

? Would more people make their own bread?

? What about people without teeth?

? At what age would a toddler have to obey the rule?

? If you ate the ingredients only would that be okay?

? Are the rule makers rule breakers?

? What if you had no money?

? Would there be new inventions of recipes for bread and things to put on bread?

? Why don't we like being told what to do?
? What reaction do we have to being told what to do?

Find the Facts and Find the Feelings

If you are talking about a topic such as bread, think about any other connections you can make to the topic, taking into account the ages of your children.

Marie Antoinette and 'Let them eat cake'

For older children the story of the French Queen Marie Antoinette, and her famous (if misquoted) words 'If they cry because they have no bread, why don't they eat cake?' can provide a different and fascinating discussion starter to Find the Facts and Find the Feelings thinking.

If your children have seen the musical *Les Misérables* or if they have read *A Tale of Two Cities* or *The Scarlet Pimpernel* or are studying the French Revolution, or even if there is press publicity about Bastille Day, you could do your own research. If you have the opportunity to travel in France, a tour of Versailles and Marie Antoinette's 'Country Village' in the palace grounds makes this period of history come to life. I fondly remember as a girl walking round the pretty, rustic buildings and later standing at those massive gates to Versailles imagining the angry throng with their pitchforks and farm implements beating on the gates and Marie Antoinette in her secluded apartment inquiring about the din.

Some questions we could ask about Marie Antoinette:

* Should she have known 'better'?
* Why didn't she understand the situation?
* Whose fault was it if she lived in 'pixie land'– an unrealistic world?
* Were her parents or husband to blame?
* Was it typical of the times?
* Was it her responsibility to know what was going on?
* Can we understand why some people were inflamed by her words?
* At what age are people responsible?

Try to find out why people think what they think. Discuss trust, believing, truth, education, influence, ignorance, knowledge, sympathy, free will, choice and greed.

Mouldy bread

Wrap a slice of bread in cling wrap and let it go mouldy. Then produce it and ask your children what it is. It may take them some time to actually figure out it is mouldy bread – fruit cake or a sponge might be mentioned, depending how colourful the mould is.

By now your children will be starting to expect the unexpected! To choruses of 'yuck!' and horror and disgust (both real and mock), say how last week you all enjoyed delicious sandwiches made from this very same bread. Ask your children if mouldy bread reminds them of other things that were good at one time, then turned bad.

Discuss things that were okay but can turn bad:

* The earth – we think it's good but there can be earthquakes
* People
* Exercise
* Jet skis
* Guns
* Charity (people can become too dependent)
* Fire
* Stories
* Myths
* Films
* Television shows
* Gambling
* Bees
* Trusting people
* Blackberries
* Medicine
* Pressure
* Knives
* Hobbies (they can take over your life)
* Electricity
* Swimming pools
* Sailing
* Rescuing people (danger to rescuers)
* Cane toads
* Rabbits
* Necklace or scarf (these can choke)
* Love (if someone doesn't love you back and breaks your heart)

Mouldy bread is a great analogy for behaviour that has 'gone off' – with just the right amount of fascination and revulsion to capture the imagination and open minds. Why does some behaviour turn bad? Some of the things that can change behaviour for the worse include: being 'silly' to be funny, because someone is confused or, because a lot of things are happening in someone's life and they are not coping, because the person is little and they don't understand. Some foods can make some people silly, friends can influence you to be silly if they are being silly, jealousy can make you say or do silly things, being scared, nervous, hot, grumpy, wanting to be popular, wanting to get attention, not wanting to feel left out, showing off can all make behaviour 'go off'.

Bread making

Make some bread with your children, and observe the yeasty dough rise like magic. Use bread making to lead your children to explore the idea that 'small things can be very important'.

Make some bread rolls. Prepare two bowls of dough. Place the same ingredients, mix and knead each bowl of dough exactly the same, but *leave out the yeast in one mixture*. Yeast is only such a tiny proportion of the mixture, after all. You're not leaving out much. Divide your mixtures into bread rolls and bake. See how important that small bit of yeast is! Half of your rolls should be fluffy, warm, fragrant and delicious. The other bread rolls will be small and hard and tough.

Discuss with your children all the small things we might take for granted but that are very important: kindness, a smile, manners and politeness.

Killer bread

Quote these 'facts' or statistics to your children, as they are about to bite into a slice of bread:

* Did you know that in our city, ninety-five percent of people who die as a result of accident or stroke have eaten bread in the month before they died?
* Did you know that there has been a hundred percent mortality rate of people who ate bread and were born in 1881?
* Ninety-one percent of people who die have eaten bread in the past six hours
* Ninety-two percent of people who need heart transplants have eaten bread daily for over thirty years
* Over three-quarters of people involved in car accidents have eaten bread regularly
* Statistics show that of all people admitted to hospital, ninety-eight percent of them have eaten bread at some time in their life
* Statistics show that ninety percent of young children admitted to hospital have eaten bread in the previous ten-hour period

All these factors prove that eating bread is a health hazard. There should be warnings printed on the bread packages!

Pretend to read these facts out of the newspaper. Be incredulous. Wait for a reaction from your children. Wait for them to splutter and spit out that mouthful of bread! Then wait for the light to dawn and get your teeth into a hearty discussion about believing.

* What if these 'statistics' were true?
* Who or what should we believe?
* Can truth or facts be used to tell a lie?
* Why are some things easy or hard to believe?
* What is a fact?
* What is 'the truth'?
* Do we believe things because others do?
* Why don't we believe some things?

* Why don't people believe and respond to warnings on cigarette packets?

Dough, bread and money

Money is sometimes referred to as 'dough' or 'bread' and you could discuss money with your children when you are thinking about bread. Otherwise a thousand opportunities come up when you can find the right time to discuss money and worth, needs and wants and so forth.

Some questions you could discuss about money include:

* What are things worth?
* What is money?
* Does money give you power?
* What if there was no money?
* Are some things priceless? What and why?
* Can you buy friends with money?
* Is stealing right if you give money from the rich to the poor as Robin Hood did?

Who would have thought that so many ideas and issues to discuss would come out of a slice of bread! It is so easy to take the everyday world for granted and forget that with a little imagination and thinking strategies, our minds can be opened by simple things.

The broken vase

Actions lie louder than words.
Carolyn Wells 1869–1942

Blame is a 'hot topic' for children. Frequently the word 'fault' appears in conversations with them. To help children to discover for themselves ideas about responsibility and blame, an interesting discussion can grow from the following stories about a broken vase. Use the thinking tools Pigeonhole It, Find the Facts, Find the Feelings, Good, Bad and Curious and What If …?

Blame and responsibility

Arrange flowers, or dust a vase and tell your children a story about it. Choose a vase with a history. Maybe it is very old or very large or maybe it has sentimental value. Share the story of your wedding and how you got the vase as a present; tell about your grandmother who owned the vase or whatever the history of the vase may be.

If you don't have a vase that is very special, use as an example anything else in your home that is breakable. Or make up a story which involves a vase.

I'm lucky to have an interesting vase story. I have a very large china vase. Made in the 1800s, it journeyed to this country in a sailing ship.

Many people had treasured and looked after the vase for nearly two centuries. This vase used to sit on the mantelpiece next to the piano in my music teacher's front room. It was a witness to all my piano lessons from the time I was eight. It witnessed my fifteen-year-old clammy hands when my music teacher's son came home from school and put his head round the door to ask, 'What's to eat, Mum?' I married my music teacher's son, and watched the vase through the years until recently the vase was given to me.

The day I was given the vase, I was delighted and placed it in pride of place with a floral display comprising several bunches of flowers. My husband and I went out for the day. Daughter Andrea went to take the dog for a walk and caught the lead in one of the flowers and brought the vase crashing to the floor. She stuck the bits of the vase together and coloured in the glued areas with coloured markers to match the colour of the vase. She then replaced the arrangement and it was a few days before I noticed the vase was broken.

This story could be told to your children as a story from a friend of yours. Lots of questions emerge from this story; questions about:

* owning up
* guilt
* value and worth … does the fact that something is broken mean that it is ruined? If someone has gone to the trouble of repairing something does that in itself mean the object is of value?
* What does precious mean? What objects would you take with you if the house caught fire and you could take just a few things with you? Why would you choose these objects?

Four breakages

Children enjoy arguing about these little anecdotes covering four different ways a vase might have been broken. The result in each case is a smashed vase. Wonder with your children who of these people should be punished? Are there degrees of responsibility, 'badness' and blame?

Jill has a party and a precious vase is smashed:

1. What if in the middle of the party the lights go out? Phil remembers seeing a torch in the kitchen but on his way to get it knocks over the vase in the dark?
2. What if in the middle of the party Mill yells, 'Look at me everybody' and does a handstand, and knocks over the vase?
3. What if in the middle of the party Bill is having a deeply philosophical discussion with some friends. He tries to explain we are all free to do anything and picks up the vase, which is nearby, and flings it to the floor to prove his point?
4. What if the next day Till, a 'friend' of Jill's, calls in to say how disappointed she is that she didn't get invited to the party. Words are exchanged, things get heated. Jill accuses Till of being nasty and hostile. 'So you think I'm hostile! I'll show you hostility!' says Till, who picks up the vase and smashes it on the floor.

How would you judge Phil, Mill, Bill and Till? Perhaps you'll think that Phil broke the vase accidentally – he was only trying to be helpful. He was observant, and was being responsible and kind. Mill on the other hand was being silly, careless, and irresponsible. She was an attention seeker.

Bill believes in different 'rights'. He deliberately broke the vase, but it was accidental in that the vase just happened to be there (a case of being in the wrong place at the wrong time). He did not deliberately set out to hurt Jill. He had an urge to do something, he was not thinking of the consequences and he was inconsiderate of others.

Till's breaking of the vase was stupid, deliberate, nasty and selfish. She did it to deliberately hurt Jill. Till was upset, mad and hurt.

Some questions to think about include:

* If you have a good reason to do something is it okay to do it?
* Was Jill responsible?
* Was it her mother's fault?
* Should the vase have been put away?
* How old were the people?
* At what age should kids be responsible?
* In Phil's case was the person who caused the accident that knocked over the power pole that caused the blackout to blame? If someone had turned off the power to the house as a joke would they be to blame?

Is it good to get angry?

Is anger a reason or an excuse for doing something bad? Let's apply the guidelines of Good, Bad and Curious to the question:

Good

✓ Healthy not to bottle things up
✓ Releases emotions
✓ Feels good
✓ People will take notice

Bad

✗ Feel bad afterwards
✗ Hurts others – friends, family and yourself
✗ Makes others angry
✗ Scares people
✗ Can make you lose friends

Curious

? Does showing anger depend on how you were brought up?
? Where do anger and manners fit?
? Do different people have different beliefs about anger?
? Should we be able to control ourselves?

Children enjoy being to be able to blame others who are 'in the wrong'. Assumptions are held but slowly the realisation dawns that things can seem the same but actually be quite different. It's interesting to look at issues that you thought were clear and obvious, and look for the reasons you believe what you do. It's fun and rewarding to work out what the differences are.

The Broken Vase story opens up many issues about responsibility and blame. These ideas can be built on, changed, revisited and adapted as instances and issues involving responsibility come up. Children find these issues important and relevant to their life. They have great fun arguing, finding examples, and trying to get to the bottom of the difference between accidentally and 'on purpose'.

Using events as keys to discussions

Anything which parents have not learned from experience they can now learn from their children.

Anonymous

Events and ceremonies provide wonderful opportunities to chase ideas with your children. You can use your own significant events as keys to chase ideas about issues. Use your travelling time to a parade to talk about ideas and have some fun thinking aloud with your children. Pigeonhole It, Find the Facts, Find the Feelings, Good, Bad and Curious and What If …? will help you to open up your topics. Use everyday events, happenings, celebrations, outings to the zoo or even getting a pet to introduce interesting, important issues to your children, which you can then discuss.

April Fool's Day

April Fool's Day is a perfect time to wonder about truth and lies, and tricks that some people might find amusing and others might find hurtful.

It is interesting to note that April Fool's Day evolved in the sixteenth century in France. In those days the new year was celebrated, with parties and dancing, in spring on the first of April. The calendar was reformed and New Year's Day was moved to the first of January (Gregorian Calendar). Some people didn't hear of the changes to the calendar, or continued to celebrate the new year on the first of April. These people were called 'fools' and were teased and ridiculed, and practical jokes and pranks were played on them.

Find the Facts

April Fool's Day is the first of April. We can trick people and tell lies until noon. After noon *you're* the fool if you trick people or tell a lie.

Find the Feelings

April Fool's Day is fun. People make up crazy, imaginative tricks, people laugh, it's fun getting tricked, it's fun tricking others, it's fun planning a trick, it's a different and special day from all the other days in the year.

Good, Bad and Curious

Good
- ✓ People laugh and lighten up
- ✓ It cheers people up
- ✓ Fun to plan and do tricks
- ✓ Good to tell stories about tricks we have played

Bad
- ✗ Tricks can be nasty
- ✗ It can ruin your day
- ✗ You can feel bad
- ✗ You can feel foolish
- ✗ People can feel cross and upset
- ✗ Some people may get injured from a silly trick that goes wrong

Curious
- ? What is trust?
- ? Who can we trust?
- ? If you're meant to tell fibs is it still a fib?
- ? Talk about truth (see page 103 on Truth and Killer Bread)

Getting a pet

You can make an opportunity to discuss issues of responsibility and animal rights when talking about pets with your children. If you're feeding a pet, or you get a new pet, you can play a game of trying to find definitions of a pet.

What is a pet?

* Is a pet an animal that loves you?
* Is a pet an animal you love?
* Is a pet an animal that can be taught tricks?
* Is a pet better than a teddy bear?
* If you love your pet and it gets very old or is in too much pain and won't get better should you have your pet put down?
* Pets, unlike farm animals, can go to training school
* Should you find out about the animal before you get one for a pet?
* What do you have to have ready before you get your pet?
* Can a wild animal be a pet?
* Your mother might call you a pet. Why?

When you have a pet you need to have the right conditions for them. You could play 'Let's Pretend' and pretend you are going to get a baby elephant, or a crocodile or a baby monkey. Discuss the needs of these animals and answer the question, 'Would these animals make good pets?'

A visit to the zoo

Next time you visit a zoo you can wonder about zoos and find Good, Bad and Curious points about them.

* You could try to judge which enclosure you think is the best enclosure and give reasons why you think this is so.
* Compare different enclosures for animals at the zoo.
* If you visit a zoo in another city you could compare the zoos.
* You could play What If …? and design your own zoo enclosures for different animals. The animals need to feel at home and people need to be able to clean the cages and also see the animals.

Animal rights

* Is it fair to keep animals in zoos?
* If a lion escaped from the zoo and was threatening a young child, would it be right to kill the lion?
* If it wasn't threatening anyone should you kill it? What other alternatives would you have?
* Is it okay for people to kill animals for food?
* Is it okay for people to kill animals for sport when the people killing the animals have plenty of food?
* In what ways are animals similar to humans?
* In what ways are animals different from humans?
* If animals are fierce or dangerous, is that a good reason to kill the animal?
* Should we kill snakes that could kill people?

A celebration of brave soldiers

Should we celebrate people who have defended their country in war time? What are some of the Good, Bad and Curious issues to be considered here?

Good

☑ Celebrate the war is over
☑ Celebrate people who have been brave and kind
☑ Remember and celebrate that they helped your country
☑ Feel lucky to be alive, lucky that others have helped your country
☑ We can celebrate that people learnt about and made medical discoveries and technological advances
☑ We can learn from the survivors of war about war
☑ We never forget
☑ We forgive
☑ We celebrate friendships made
☑ We are reminded to appreciate peace

Bad

✘ Brings back bad memories for some people who went to war
✘ Feel sad about the loss of friends and loved ones

X   Remember that families were destroyed or loved ones were killed or lost

X   Remember death, pain and loss, people maimed for life, innocent people suffering, starving people, children losing childhood, people's lives affected forever, buildings, bridges, art and historical treasures destroyed, crops and countryside ruined

Curious

? Are we celebrating war or celebrating people who tried to help others?

? Did some people enlist not knowing what they were going to be involved with?

? Why did people enlist? (Belief in tradition and honour, duty as a citizen)

? Did some people go to war willingly because they loved their country?

? How would it feel if you were forced to kill people because you were a soldier?

? What if you refused to fight and kill people?

? Why do people have good and bad memories of war?

? Is there a difference between fighting to take land from someone else and fighting to protect your own land?

? Is forgiving good?

? Will people never forget?

? Do some people want revenge?

? What about land mines as weapons of war?

? Should there be talking and resolution instead of war?

? What can the rest of the world do to stop some countries fighting?

? Why do wars start?

? Who benefits from war?

? Are the people who invent bad things (for example the atom bomb) responsible for the horrors it brings?

? Is technology always good?

? Why is there no peace in the world?

? Can something bad (bomb on Hiroshima) be good (ended the war)?

? Does the end justify the means?

? What if you don't want to kill people?
? What if people do dreadful things and use as an excuse, 'I was only doing my job – I was carrying out orders'?

Duck shooting season

When newspapers have articles about the duck shooting season (perhaps a conflict of opinion is brought out), use this as an opportunity to discuss freedom and rights with your children. If you have already discussed war, you can link ideas to points you have previously discussed. Consider the Good, Bad and Curious issues.

Good

☑ Fun for the shooters
☑ Sport
☑ Demonstrate shooting skill
☑ Believe that ducks are pests because they eat the farmer's crops – help the farmers

Bad

☒ Not fair for ducks
☒ Other birds are shot by mistake
☒ Ducks may not be killed outright by the bullets and they die in agony
☒ Endangered birds are shot

Curious

? What is a sport?
? What is tradition?
? Should people have the right to own guns?
? Many people collect ornaments with ducks on them. Why?
? Have ducks become a modern symbol for country homeliness?
? What do ducks represent? (Freedom, warmth, the country, homely kitchen)
? Describe ducks (Delicate, fragile, innocent, harmless, peaceful quiet, cute, beautiful)
? What do we consider beautiful and why? (Ducks' simple, pleasing shape may be a reason why they appeal)

Find the Facts and Find the Feelings

Pretend to be a reporter for the local newspaper interviewing the local duck shooting club to find out why they went duck shooting. Some of the reasons for people going duck shooting include:

* For delicious food
* Because shooting is enjoyable, it's a challenge
* I can show off my skill
* It's a sport
* My friends all go shooting – peer group pressure
* It's a tradition in my family
* It feels good to kill
* I get rid of my anger
* It gives me a buzz being up in the early morning with the beautiful still water, the sunrise, my gun, the excitement and anticipation, proving myself
* I'm bored with my life and look forward to the duck season to give my life a boost
* I feel powerful
* It's a competition
* I can relax when I am shooting
* Ducks are a pest because they eat farmers' crops
* Ducks need to be killed
* I'm addicted to it
* As a symbol that it's a free world and I can do what I want
* It's a game grown-ups can play

The Olympic Games

The Olympic Games provide plenty of ideas to discuss with your children. There are issues of winning and losing, drug-taking, cheating, fairness, junketing and excessive spending, ticket sales, what to do with the homeless during the Games, the cost of putting on the Games and priorities against other needs in the community.

Good

☑ Brings people together

☑ People make new friends
☑ Helps understanding and peace in the world
☑ Feels good to win – medal
☑ Glory
☑ Money from sponsors
☑ Opportunity – for fun, challenge, competition
☑ Find the best in the world
☑ Can be good sports
☑ Celebration of sport, peace and life
☑ Brings countries together
☑ Excitement
☑ Tradition and sense of history – Greek origins
☑ Personal best
☑ Fitness
☑ Exhilaration

Bad

☒ Cheating
☒ Drugs
☒ Hurting each other
☒ Heartache of not winning
☒ Anxiety
☒ Jet lag from long-distance travel
☒ Getting used to the bitter cold or hot conditions
☒ Being sick
☒ Getting disqualified if a piece of equipment fails
☒ Bad sportsmanship
☒ May wreck your body by trying too hard
☒ Other people's expectations, including coaches

Curious

? Is it a risk to be a famous sports star?
? What about things that go wrong?
? How do people deal with winning and losing?
? What is a 'good sport'?
? Would you feel you have to win for your country or is it simply good enough just to be in the Olympic team?
? Why do people want to know who the best in the world is?

? The record time doesn't last long before someone sets a new one. How would this affect the previous champion?

? Are the Winter Olympics more dangerous because the snow and ice, being slippery, makes races faster?

? How would you feel if you didn't win?

? Are the Olympics good because they give competitors something to aim for?

? Why do people push themselves too hard?

Discuss the notion of personal best

List things you do your personal best for:

* Setting the table correctly
* Manners
* Learning my times tables
* When I play sport
* Playing a musical instrument

Discuss examples of 'bad sports'

* People who boss
* People who are rude
* People who hurt other people's feelings
* People who fight, sulk, cause trouble
* People who want to be first all the time and won't take turns
* People who are pushy, throw tantrums, don't share
* People who deliberately make other people jealous
* People who quarrel or are greedy
* People who boast
* People who show off
* People who tell you your special things aren't that good

What is fair?

✳ Is taking performance-enhancing drugs fair?

✳ When is a race not fair?

✳ Why is cheating unfair?

✳ If you have murdered someone, or if you have hurt a rival on purpose, should you be allowed in the Olympic Games?

✳ What are the differences between excuses and reasons why Olympic competitors did not do their best?

✳ Some people want a race rerun so they can have another chance to race. What would be a fair reason? If your necklace got stuck in your glasses? If your toes were cold? If the wind was bad? If your ski became unclipped? If someone threw something at you? If the track was rough? If there was someone in the way? If you lost your nerve? If you lost control? If you were nervous? If there was a toddler on the track?

Events from birthday celebrations to school sports, festivals to public holidays can provide the topic and the opportunity to discuss issues with children. This way you move from comfort zones that are familiar to your children, and within no time you will find yourself embarking upon complex discussions on ethical issues, that really stretch your brains. Have fun talking about all the fascinating ideas that are hidden in events.

Finding stories in books and films

The best effect of any book is that it excites the reader to self activity.
Thomas Carlyle 1795–1881

Stories entertain. Stories open up the world to us. Stories open us up to the world. Stories allow us to understand more about life and ourselves.

Stories play an important role in chasing ideas. When you read or tell your children stories, or when they relate and tell stories of their own, they will become immersed in the thoughts held in the stories. They will be introduced to new ideas and new language, to wonder about and discuss.

A recent newspaper article stated that most children in Britain were missing out on a bedtime story. Sixty percent of children did not have a bedtime story compared with just seven percent of their parents' generation. Anecdotal evidence suggests that busy lifestyles, combined with videos and computer games, means that there is no time for bedtime stories. The result may be a lack of intimacy between children and parents.

From the time when you read your children picture storybooks, to when your children are older and reading 'chapter' books on their own, tap into this valuable resource. Stories are living, breathing ideas. Discuss the ideas in the stories, read between the lines, ask questions, find similar ideas, make links and connections, play with ideas, have fun exploring ideas.

Tell your children stories about your own childhood. Stories about how things were similar, how things were different, when you were naughty, when you got into trouble, the holidays and highlights of your life. Share these valuable memories with your child.

Stories grow discussions with our children

* Stories can touch our lives
* Stories can inspire us
* Stories can be entertaining, they can comfort us and they can teach us things
* Stories provide a framework to hold notions and ideas of Big Important Concepts
* Stories open up ideas
* Stories are a link between adults and children, children and adults
* Stories contain elements of 'play' and adventure and exploration
* Stories can be built on, altered, used in many ways to fit the age and the life's experience of the child
* Stories can be told anywhere
* Stories provide examples of varied vocabulary

Books

Read your children books you enjoyed reading when you were a child. Share your favourite stories with them.

Fairy stories, fables and proverbs

Read these stories with your young children and discuss some of the issues embedded in the story. Don't forget to look at the illustrations, as these can be important in telling the story.

There is an abundance of issues embedded in fairy stories and fables. For example:

* *The Boy Who Cried Wolf* opens up issues of lies and believing
* *The Donkey and the Shadow* opens up issues of ownership
* *The Lion and the Mouse* opens up issues of judging, friendship, believing, kindness
* *The Dog and the Bone* opens up issues of greed, imagining and loss

* *The Pied Piper of Hamelin* opens up issues of promises, breaking promises, punishment, adults and children
* *Pinocchio* opens up issues of truth, lies, and punishment
* *Cinderella* opens up issues about getting what you deserve, kindness, and unkindness
* *The Princess and the Pea* opens up issues of truth, lies, imagination, the way we judge people and differences
* *The Emperor's New Clothes* opens up issues of truth, lies, bravery and foolishness.

Picture storybooks

There is a wide selection of picture storybooks to share with your children. Discuss the characters. Find the issues and ideas in the books you read with your children. Find the ideas about seeing and believing, truth and lies, friends and enemies, cruelty and kindness, understanding and judging, dreaming and imagination, judging and punishment, fear and bravery and friends and enemies.

Fantasy books

These books open up many issues you can discuss with your children. Talk to your children about good and evil, sympathy and empathy, belonging and not belonging, mystery, magic and spells, friendship, warnings, tricks and traps and growing up. In many fantasy books characters can fly, for example in J.K. Rowling's Harry Potter books.

Use the Good, Bad and Curious thinking tool to discuss: What if I could fly?

Good

- ☑ I would be free to go wherever I want to go
- ☑ I wouldn't need to be driven places by Mum and Dad
- ☑ I could have fun flying
- ☑ I could escape from trouble by flying away
- ☑ It would be great for playing chasing games
- ☑ I could walk up high on buildings and play equipment
- ☑ I could get over any fence

Bad

- ☒ I could fall and hurt myself
- ☒ If I'm the only person able to fly, would I feel lonely?
- ☒ Would it be hard to control myself when I'm flying?
- ☒ Would my friends want me to run errands for them?

Curious

- ✳ How would I fly – would I have wings or flap my arms or fly on a broomstick?
- ✳ Would flying make walking seem slow?
- ✳ I wouldn't need to use a ladder or steps
- ✳ How would I learn to fly?
- ✳ If I had wings it could be difficult to sit on chairs because the wings would get in the way

* Would it be uncomfortable in bed if I had wings?
* Clothes would have to be different to allow my wings to poke out
* Lots of things fly and don't have wings (time, hot air balloons, clouds, imagination, ghosts, helicopters, Superman, parachutes, comets, shooting stars, spiders)
* Some birds have wings and can't fly (emus, flamingos, penguins)
* Some unusual things have wings (flying fish, wishing chair, Pegasus, Asterix)

Roald Dahl's books

Whether you read the books or see the movies these stories have many interesting notions to discuss.

The Magic Finger

* Do you think the family learnt something from their experience?
* Do you think they needed to be taught a lesson? Why?
* What do you think of hunting as a sport?
* If you had a 'magic finger' how would you use it?

Fantastic Mr Fox

* What do you think of hunting and foxhunting as a sport?
* Is it right that Mr Fox steals? Do you think that he steals?
* How does he explain his actions?
* Is it always wrong to steal?

George's Marvellous Medicine

* What can medicines do to people's bodies and minds?
* Can pills change people's thoughts?
* Why might old people feel cranky?
* What is a drug? Is it medicine?

Danny, Champion of the World

* What did Danny do to be champion of the world?
* Can bad things (a broken leg) make things turn out for the better?
* Are you glad when his plan to get his pheasants works, even if it is wrong?
* Poaching is illegal. Were Danny and his father right or wrong in what they did?

Matilda

* What's Matilda's safety valve? Why does she need a safety valve?
* What is your safety valve?
* What did Matilda's parents think about girls and boys?
* Do you agree or disagree with them?

Films

Movies and films capture our imagination and influence our ideas. My editor, Bryony, told me about the effect the movie *Toy Story* had on her daughter Emma, who after seeing the movie (which contained scenes about the disappointment of discarded toys) refused to throw anything away. Films can have a profound effect on children. I wonder if you were frightened out of your wits when you first saw the *Wizard of Oz*. I was. Those witches really terrified me; I also longed to have a pair of red sparkly shoes like Dorothy's. The *Star Wars* movies put forward the notion of a force for good and captured the imagination of a generation. *The Sound of Music* is still screened as family entertainment in the parks during summer in large cities throughout the world. These and other movies provide serendipitous opportunities to discuss the issues raised in them.

Going out to see a movie also means that you have great opportunities to talk about the movie while you're eating at the  restaurant, walking to the cinema or travelling home, so talk about the plot and the actors and the scenery and the special effects. Discuss whether the film was a thriller or a comedy or a fantasy. Compare the film to similar films you have seen. Pigeonhole It. Compare similar films; which film worked best for you? Why do you prefer that film?

Perhaps it's the size, or the sound, or simply the 'treat' angle of taking our children to the cinema but use your movie-going as an opportunity to grow discussions with them. Of course, videos are another way to share stories with children.

Ideas you may find in films to discuss with your children include: families, belonging, jealousy, beliefs, right and wrong, hope, judging others, being a failure, unreal expectations, bravery, courage, fear, things that scare us, being kind and good and evil.

Make up your own moral for the story such as:

* You don't have to let others tell you what to do
* Make up your own mind
* Do what *you* think is right
* You can't trust everyone
* You get what you deserve
* United we stand, divided we fall

You could make up your own new titles for the book or film.

Stories from books and films can be used as keys to open up many issues that are important to think about and understand. Children can't understand *all* about ownership or rights or responsibilities, but a backbone or framework will develop on which to attach other thoughts about the idea, as more examples become apparent.

By helping children to develop their own backbone of concepts about important issues, we help them choose and judge issues that involve themselves. The thesaurus defines backbone as 'spine, fortitude, character, determination, integrity, firmness, courage, guts and resolution'. We want our children to have backbone; we want them to have all of these characteristics.

Using the media

The most important services rendered by the press and the magazines is that of educating people to approach printed matter with distrust.

Samuel Butler 1835–1902

Encourage your children from an early age to look through newspapers. The print media, television and films, influence the way our children think. We can use the media as a great source for discussion with children. Use the thinking tools of Pigeonhole It, Find the Facts, Find the Feelings, Good, Bad and Curious and What If ...? to open up issues.

We can discuss if the media manipulates the way we think. In newspapers we can look at headlines, pictures, and articles to consider if what is presented is a fact, or an opinion. Who is the target audience? We can examine the content of news reports about events and people at a local or worldwide level. We can do similar detective work about magazines, especially looking at the interests of the readers.

Discuss with your children where we get 'news' from: word-of-mouth, radio, television, the Internet, and newspapers.

Television

Ask your children, 'What is television?'. 'Du-u-r!' I can hear their reply. But think about it and I'm sure you'll come up with all sorts of answers, from a piece of furniture to a means of mass communication. It can also be a status symbol (that huge screen), entertainment on tap, an influencer and shaper of society, a dream machine, a tranquilliser, a child minder, a diverter, a hobby, a time waster and a treat!

Watch different types of programs with your children and Pigeonhole It or classify the programs that you watch. For example, was it fact, opinion, news, entertainment, a nonfiction film or a film about a true story, a documentary or real life television? How many different pigeonholes can you find for programs? Jot your suggestions down in your Thinking Trap Resource Book, talk and argue about which classification a program fits. Maybe it fits into several of your classifications.

Stories that appear in the news can be also used as keys to discuss issues with your children.

The following examples show the sorts of discussions that can grow out of a newspaper article or news program. Children love to discuss 'real' issues, particularly if their friends are aware of the same issues.

Baby show

Two mothers fought at a baby show. They punched each other because both mothers thought that their baby was the best baby in the competition. Some questions might be:

* How can you judge the 'best' baby? (Is it the baby who is quiet? The baby who is wearing the 'best' clothes? Well trained? Has the most hair?)
* Is there such a thing as the 'best' baby?
* Would everyone choose the same baby?
* What about the baby who is well behaved at the show but not when at home?
* Is the 'best' baby at the show a reflection of the 'truth'?
* While the mums were fighting, what happened to the babies?
* How would the dads feel when they learnt that their wives were fighting over who had the best baby? (Find the Feelings)
* Name other competitions that are held. (Pigeonhole It)
* What categories (for example speed, beauty and knowledge) can competitions have?
* Are baby shows typical of competitions?

* What competitions do your children participate in?
* Discuss competitions using the Good, Bad and Curious thinking tool.

Flying girl

Jessica, a seven-year-old American girl, crashed her plane and died. She was flying in stormy conditions. She had her flying instructor with her, and he also died. Reports show she had a very unusual childhood with no normal toys. She was trying to get into the *Guinness Book of Records*.

Find the Facts

* Weather was bad
* Plane was overloaded
* Jessica was so small she had to have a special seat

Find the Feelings

* We feel cross if her parents pushed her to fly
* We feel sad that a young life was lost
* Did she die fulfilling a dream?

Pigeonhole It

* Can a seven-year-old be well enough informed about flying conditions to make the right decisions?
* What sorts of decisions are suitable for a seven-year-old to make?

* Why does the law stop seven-year-olds driving a car on the road?
* Why doesn't the law stop seven-year-olds flying a plane?

Curious

* Did her parents want her to be famous?
* Is she more famous because she died?
* The *Guinness Book of Records* stopped recording records with kids because of her
* Did her parents push her because of money?
* Why do people try to break records?
* Are people influenced by famous people?

* Who is to blame? Parents, Jessica (Are we responsible at seven years of age?), aviation authorities who knew that the weather would be bad but let her go, the *Guinness Book of Records*, the instructor, the press?
* Could Jessica have refused to go?
* Did they break the flying rules?
* Should we follow our dream no matter how dangerous it is?

Sailor lost at sea

Quite often we read or hear about people who are rescued. It is wonderful when people can be saved. Are there other issues to consider?

Not so long ago, two million dollars were spent to rescue an adventuring, lone woman sailor. She had suffered a mishap and become lost at sea. She was participating in a round-the-world race.

Good

☑ Human life is worth more than money
☑ The rescue was good publicity for the rescuing country
☑ Sailors who find themselves in trouble in waters belonging to other countries can expect to be rescued by the nearest country
☑ The rescue was a valuable experience for the rescue teams and defence forces to check that their systems work

Bad

✗ Danger to the rescuers
✗ A great deal of money is spent on one person
✗ The money would have been better spent on street kids, medical research, helping victims of flood or other disasters

Curious

? If it is the law to save sailors in our waters should this law be obeyed?
? If lives are put in danger with a yacht or car race should the race be held?
? Is it the sailor's responsibility because she chose to be in the race?
? Is it the organisers' responsibility?

? Is the nationality of the people we rescue important?
? If a person who had paid taxes to the country was rescued would that feel fair?
? Should the sailor or her family pay for the rescue?
? Should her country pay for the rescue?
? Should we only rescue certain people? Should it depend on who the person is?
? How can we judge the worth of a person?
? Is it different if she made a mistake and went off course or if her equipment was faulty?
? What should the priorities be for spending money from taxes?
? Should we treat others how we'd like to be treated?

Dealing with terrorists

There are regular media reports about terrorists. By taking people hostage, threatening to destroy planes and planting poison in food, terrorists make demands of organisations and governments, who have to try to deal with such threats. Accepting the demands of terrorists can have huge ramifications.

Good

☑ Saves the lives of innocent people
☑ Stops the terrorists doing worse things if they are ignored

Bad

✗ Does this encourage other people to become terrorists?
✗ What if you have to free a bad person from jail?

Curious

? Does the end always justify the means?
? Are the demands just a bluff?
? What would the terrorists think about what they are doing? What priorities do they see?
? What are the priorities of organisations and governments?
? What is negotiation?
? What is compromise?
? What are some other examples of negotiation and compromise?

Adventurers

Young people like to go on amazing adventures. Frequently these people have the thrill of a lifetime. At other times things can go wrong, such as the flash flood in Switzerland, when people body-surfing down a canyon were drowned.

Good

✓ Young and strong
✓ Fun
✓ Experience of a lifetime
✓ Thrills, adrenaline rush
✓ Sense of adventure
✓ Pit themselves against nature
✓ Feel wonderful and strong
   afterwards

Bad

✗ Dangerous thing to do
✗ Weather changes can create
   extra dangers
✗ Rescuers lives were put in
   danger
✗ Can be terrible conditions
   for rescuers
✗ Money spent on search
✗ Terrible time for families
✗ There might be criticism
   of search teams

Curious

? If you are lost, is holding onto hope that rescue will come the most important thing?
? Should people eat dead bodies if there is nothing else to eat and otherwise they would die?
? Is it better for one person to have a chance to live, by being given all the food and water?
? How would you choose which person should live or to die?

? Is the moment when you give up the moment when you will be found?

? Does the unexpected happen?

Adventurer in the desert

We shouldn't believe everything we read or see. The media can manipulate stories to capture people's interest, sell more newspapers, and attract more viewers. The next story is an example of media manipulation.

Robert Bogucki, an Alaskan fireman/adventurer, was lost in the West Australian desert for forty days. It was reported he was seeking out God. Many people searched for him but he was found by a television channel's helicopter. The reporters on the helicopter landed, gave him a banana to eat and filmed him being sick. They had to leave one of their reporters at the water hole where they found Bogucki because of the weight in the helicopter. They did not notify the authorities that they had found Bogucki. They did not take him to hospital until they had interviewed him to get a 'scoop' story. Bogucki had lost more than twenty-seven kilograms from his ordeal in the desert.

It seemed to many who read this story that media manipulation had occurred. Discuss with your children whether they thought the media acted 'honourably' and analyse what the media should have done instead.

Find the Feelings

How do you feel when you hear this story?

* Sad
* Mad
* Bad
* Cross
* Relieved
* Happy because the man has been found
* Upset
* Confused
* Disgruntled with the television channel

Good

- ☑ He survived
- ☑ He was found alive
- ☑ Chance to tell and sell his story
- ☑ Famous
- ☑ Money for him
- ☑ He will treasure life
- ☑ Television channel news scoop
- ☑ People interested
- ☑ Will there be medical discoveries because he has lasted so long without food?
- ☑ Is this a good warning for people?

Bad

- ☒ Lots of money, time and effort spent on the search
- ☒ Hard work for searchers
- ☒ He lost a lot of weight – will this affect his health in the future?
- ☒ Worrying time for family
- ☒ Will the television channel be sued?
- ☒ Newsman left behind as not enough room in the helicopter

Curious

- ☐ Was he really searching for God as reported?
- ☐ Why would you find God in the desert?
- ☐ Did he avoid the searchers?
- ☐ Why didn't he realise people would be looking for him?
- ☐ Should he pay for the search?
- ☐ Was he asking for trouble?
- ☐ What helped him to survive?
- ☐ Is he rich? (Should he pay half the money for the search?)
- ☐ Was he smart?
- ☐ Did he find God?
- ☐ Was this all for attention?
- ☐ Is this man brave or foolish?
- ☐ Did the television channel plan all this to get viewers? (Was it a con or practical joke?)
- ☐ Does he need the money?

? Should he get the money?
? Why didn't he 'get lost' in Alaska, his own country?
? Did he have personal troubles?
? Does he deserve to be famous and influence others?
? Why is he called an 'adventurer'?
? Does it matter that one man lives?
? Is it fair spending so much money on the search for one man?
? Did it make any difference that he was not Australian?
? Is it fair that Australians spend their tax money on him?
? Should we be allowed to choose to die?
? Can we believe the facts?
? Is there such a thing as truth?
? Will he donate the money he gets from media to a good cause or pay back the search money?
? Would we be searched for if we went missing?
? Will there be copycats who think he did a smart thing?
? Are the newspapers hiding material or are they showing us all they know?
? Are newspapers good or bad?

What If ...?

* Should people have to take beeper, mobile phone or flare when going out to sea or into harsh country?
* How can we invent some things that would have helped him or people lost in the snow?
* What are the similarities and differences between him and people lost in the snow?
* What rules should there be for people going out to sea or into harsh country?

Advertising

Wherever you are, you will see advertising and commercials. You can use advertising to chase ideas and reason with your children. Play the What If ...? game: choose the goods you would have if you could have what you want. Use advertisements so that you can discuss and point out the difference between needs and wants.

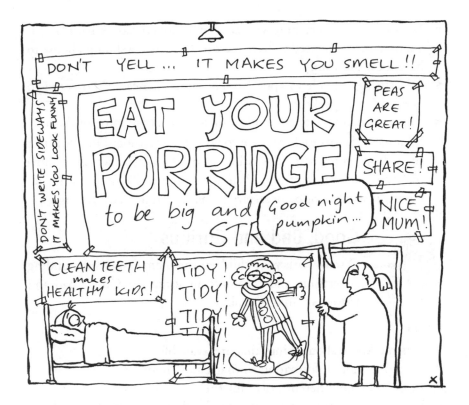

Because there is so much advertising in our lives we can use it to provide opportunities for judging and decision-making. Discuss the ads you see, try to work out what their message is, what methods are used to get the message across, let your children be aware of tricks and strategies used. Look at the difference between fact and fantasy, exaggeration and truth.

Find the Facts

* The influence of advertising comes through radio and television, posters, printed catalogues and brochures, newspapers and magazines and on the Internet.
* Business relies on advertising to let people know about their products and services.
* Advertising is based on persuasion, influencing us to change our lives by having different products.

* We can't have everything we see that is advertised. Advertising is about choice. We need to have reasons for why we should choose to have a certain thing.
* Advertising is made to appeal to certain audiences. Who is the ad designed to appeal to?
* There are many messages implied in ads. What are some of them?
* Billions of dollars each year are spent on advertising. Does this fact show how important advertising is or does this fact show how ineffective advertising really is? (If it were more effective in influencing us, it would not be necessary to have so much advertising.)

Good, Bad and Curious

Discuss with your children the many issues surrounding advertising and commercials using the Good, Bad and Curious thinking tool.

Good

☑ Lets me know about things that are available
☑ Gives me more information so that I can choose
☑ I can compare different prices for the same articles
☑ I can cut out ads and take them to the shops to compare goods
☑ Makes me aware of things I might not otherwise know
☑ Some of the images are interesting and attractive
☑ Makes money for advertisers
☑ Provides jobs for artists, designers, film crews and photographers
☑ Makes money for the sponsors because people buy things
☑ Makes money for the television and radio stations, and magazines and newspapers because time on air or space is paid for
☑ Can be community advertising (promote road safety, encourage a more caring society) or asking for money for charities
☑ Money that comes from advertising means that television channels can provide more programs

Bad

✗ Can be irritating (fills up television programs and newspapers and magazines)
✗ Can make me want things I didn't know I wanted

✘ Can be boring, especially if the ad is frequently repeated
✘ Can be ridiculous and tell nothing about the product being promoted
✘ Can have 'hidden' messages
✘ Can have stereotypes so I feel I should have certain things, be slim, or dress in a certain way to be 'cool'
✘ Can make me dissatisfied with my car, clothes or house
✘ Can make me feel dissatisfied with my life as it seems boring compared with the lives of people in the advertisements
✘ Advertising costs a lot of money, and the buying public has to cover these costs
✘ Advertising can make suggestions that may be harmful for us and promote some goods such as confectionery as healthy
✘ Brochures use huge amounts of paper
✘ Advertising on paper can be discarded and make litter
✘ Promotions about new shows on television can be particularly irritating

Curious

? Does advertising control our thinking?
? Do ads always 'tell the truth'? Can we always believe what advertising tells us? If an advertisement says it's good, does that mean it must be good?
? Find an example of a 'good' ad and a 'bad' ad. Explain why you think they are good or bad.
? What is a sponsor? What do they want?
? What is the difference between a lie and twisting the truth or openly exaggerating a statement?
? What about 'banner ads' from advertisers on the Internet? Is this fair?
? Can advertising affect the way news is reported? (If the advertiser is a big paying customer would this influence reporting about something bad the company has done?)
? What about cash for comments (where a television or radio personality is paid money to make favourable comments about a product), if the public is unaware that money has been paid?
? What about sponsorship of athletes?

? Imagine you are an athlete and you rely on having a sponsor. What if you find out that people who make the products you have to endorse work in bad or dangerous conditions?

? When does advertising become propaganda attempting to change the views of a large group of people?

Discussing the pros and cons of advertising can seem like a P2C2E (Process Too Complicated to Explain) but as you nibble away at issues, your children can be building a framework of ideas to build on, to help them judge and

make choices. It's impossible to discuss all these ideas about the media in one sitting, or even a day or week. But you can build up layers of knowledge and ideas gradually as issues become obvious or important. Bit by bit add to your children's file of understanding about the media. Use the media to open up your children's eyes. Help them to think and be aware.

Thinking tools can help you out

17

Life is mostly froth and bubble,
Two things stand like stone —
Kindness in another's trouble,
Courage in your own.

Adam L. Gordon 1833–1870

Chasing ideas and thinking aloud builds self-respect and confidence. Once your children are familiar with the five thinking tools, (the Handy Thinking tools), and have had practice using the various tools on a variety of topics, they can adapt the tools to creatively 'see' and understand issues. *The following topics are most important to think aloud about. They are more than merely 'curious', or 'interesting'.*

Remind your children they always have their Handy Thinking tools to help them out. They can always find a way to crack open an issue or think about a problem. Prompt them to use these thinking tools when they look baffled. Let them jog your memory and remind you to use your thinking tools if you look perplexed.

If they have used the Handy Thinking tools, they will remember that to tackle any problem, the first thing they have to do is find out what sort of category the problem fits into. They need to point out the facts and reflect about how the various people involved in the problem think and feel. Work out the Good, Bad and Curious issues and wonder What If …? about various ways of tackling the problem and the consequences of the action.

> How you cope depends on one thing – what you think!

Here are some important ideas to draw out. You can let the discussions wander, but try to bring your discussions back to these major points.

Heroes

Media articles provide opportunities to discuss heroes. Discuss brave, courageous people using Find the Feelings thinking. Give your children examples of courageous deeds, chase ideas about what it would feel like if you were in the situation the person was in. In your Thinking Trap Resource Book, keep a list of people whom you think are brave with the reason why they were brave. Recognise all the different ways people are courageous, include family members and friends' names in your list. Don't forget to put your children's names on the list when they do something brave.

Courage comes from our ideas and our self-talk. Knowledge is power – knowledge about the situation and knowledge about the different coping strategies we can use.

Rembember, triumph is made up of two words, 'try' and 'umph'. To triumph through difficult times we must try and have plenty of umph. We also need perseverance and persistence, goal setting and re-evaluating of these goals.

Courage can be seen as 'coeur' (French for heart) and 'rage': Courage is rage of the heart. We need this rage of the heart to face our fears and disappointments and to move forward with hope.

Coping

Point out your coping strategies to your children. Help them uncover their coping strategies so they can build up their own ways to cope. It is important to tackle issues *before* they arise so that children will be armed with knowledge and strategies.

Here are some comments from children about what helps them to cope.

* I've discovered that *talking* to somebody really helps
* I *write down* my problems and different alternatives I have
* I get help from *Mum and Dad* or my teachers

* I *work* really hard
* I just *worry*
* I stay with my *friends*
* I *daydream*
* I find *other people who have similar problems*
* I eat or I *slam the door*
* I *keep my mind occupied* with different things ... I try to forget my worries
* I *shut myself in my room* – this allows me a breathing space, but it is just a brief escape
* I think about the good things and *concentrate on the positive things*.
* I escape by *playing games* on the computer
* I find that *running* helps me relax

Courage is needed to cope with competition and also to cope with jealousy. Discuss issues of competition or jealousy with your children when the time seems appropriate.

We need courage to face our fears and disappointments. We also need courage to dare, dream and hope.

Bullying

Bullying is often covered by the media, whether it be of an apprentice tormented by workmates or long-term bullying at a school. Use a newspaper report to open up the issue of bullying and discuss it with your children so that you already have a framework of ideas (jotted in your Thinking Trap) to revisit if your child is bullied.

Find the Facts

Dictionary definition of bullying: When a person takes pleasure in hurting or intimidating a weaker person. Dictionary definition of intimidate: to scare, frighten or discourage someone.

Curious issues to consider

* Is bullying a habit?
* Is it because the bullies have no manners?
* Are crooks bullies?
* Some bullies seem to bully to get attention
* Some people don't even know they are bullying
* Sometimes what looks like bullying can be an accident
* For some people bullying is like a game

Find the Feelings

Why do bullies bully?

* Sometimes they've been bullied by their parents or brothers and sisters so they think it's normal
* Sometimes they're taking it out on someone else because they're confused or stressed
* Sometimes because they're jealous
* Sometimes for revenge
* Sometimes because they 'lose it' – they can't control their temper
* Sometimes because they like to see you cry
* Sometimes to be heroes to younger kids
* Sometimes they think it makes them popular
* Sometimes because they think it makes them look 'cool' (and anti-social)
* Sometimes they seem to think that aggression, popularity and control go together
* Sometimes to make you feel small so they feel big

Curious

? Bullying can be hurting people physically or hurting them with words
? It can be a look
? It can be body language – a gesture or just not including people in a group
? Sometimes bullies make you give them your Mars Bar or make you do things for them, sometimes they can even stop you walking or sitting somewhere

? Bullying can depend on who you are with, and their standards – what is 'normal' to some people is 'bullying' to others. Bullies can be smart (and con people) or dumb

? Can you 'catch' bullying and copy bullies or are we all born with a little bit of bullying in us?

? People do all sorts of things to cope with bullying

? Some people slurp and try to be friends with bullies some act like a bully, too. Some tell an older sister or brother but are told they are 'being too sensitive' or 'not tough enough' or 'It's all part of growing up!' (When sisters and brothers try to defend younger children from bullies, sometimes it only leads to more bullying and teasing)

? Some children tell their parents but feel bad troubling them because they seem to have lots of worries

? Telling a teacher can make you feel like a dobber; it may only help for a little while and you can't complain every day

? Some children try to ignore it while some children pretend and daydream about nasty things happening to bullies – they are bullied by a giant, they cop it, the teacher sees how nasty they are, they get expelled.

Some thoughts about bullying

* 'I look and feel stupid, I seem to make a fool of myself.'
* 'I try to be a good kind person but the bullies don't see it: I'm not weak, I try to be polite!'
* 'It's good to share problems and not feel alone.'
* 'Bullies seem to be able to see right through me – they can see what I think and feel – it makes me mad!'
* 'I've tried running away from the bullies, hitting them back, avoiding them, trying to get an adult to help me: there are many ways people bully so there must be many ways to deal with them.'

Compile your own statements about how to cope with bullying.

* Everyone has the right to feel safe. That includes *me*
* Many kids have problems with bullying
* I don't have to be perfect – everyone makes mistakes. I have the right to make a mistake and not be made into a dork by the bullies

* Maybe I need to lighten up a little – grow a thicker skin
* If I can look for good things rather than bad things I might feel a bit better
* I can concentrate on bullies and fairness too much
* I know I'm a worry wart – I have to be careful not to let little things get me down
* I must remember there is hope – I won't always have these bullies!
* I need to relax and divert myself: getting active, reading a book, drawing, playing a computer game is better than worrying and being upset!
* I can learn new ways of coping with bullying

Ways to cope with bullying

* *Believe that everyone has the right not to be bullied.* I am not 'imagining things' or 'blowing things out of proportion' I have the right to feel safe! No-one has the right to bully!
* *Explain things clearly.* I might have to write down some notes so that I can explain myself clearly. Sometimes when I try to explain I forget or get embarrassed and feel I have to say 'it really doesn't matter' when it really does!
* *Talk to Mum and Dad,* friends, brothers and sisters, aunts or uncles or neighbours
* *Speak to my teacher* and explain how my life is being made miserable by bullying
* *Spend time with friends* who will not laugh when bullies pick on me. Being in a *group of friends* makes me feel stronger
* When I have bullying on my mind *I keep myself busy* so I forget
* I must remember *there is always something I can do*
* I can learn to cope by *using my brains*

Encourage your children to be courageous in the way they look at others, themselves, new ideas and new experiences.

When things don't seem fair

If you have discussed the Olympic Games with your children you will have started to build a framework of 'fair' and 'winning' and 'losing'. Build on your framework by discussing the following story.

Richard Hatch won one million dollars on the television show *Survivor*, in which a group of people were taken to a tropical island. Each week someone from the group was voted off the island. The person who remained won one million dollars. Richard Hatch was seen as the 'bad' guy within the group.

If your family was dumped on a tropical island what would be some of the problems to face?

* Finding food, water and shelter
* Making a bed
* Getting on with everyone
* Working out what to do about a toilet
* Working out priorities
* Considering dangers and balancing being safe and having fun
* Feeling cut off from the world and alone
* Getting sick or hurt

* Coping with boredom
* Coping with the fear of the 'unknown'

In competitions, what characteristics do we want the winner to have? It might be being kind and helpful, accepting others, being a good sport, honest, uncritical, thinking of others, making things fun, being inventive, being friendly and not being jealous.

What characteristics would we expect the loser to have? Uncooperative, unhelpful, disrespectful, selfish, bully, brag, show off, boss, rude, cheat, nasty, breaking promises, uncaring about others, and greediness are all possibilities.

Good, Bad and Curious

Why did the 'bad' guy win? He was smart, a good judge of character and he plotted and planned. He followed his plan.

Some questions to discuss

* Was it luck that he won? What is luck?
* Was it fair? What does 'fair' mean?
* Should we expect the best or the worst from people?
* If we landed on the island should we prepare a camp site and food and then play; or should we have fun and *then* do the work?
* If you were in *Survivor* and you did something nice just so people would like you and not vote you off is that really genuine?
* Should you pretend to be nice when you're not or act as you really are?
* Was it fate that he won?
* Are you happier if you believe in fate?
* Does the end justify the means?

As your children become more aware of issues, they can look at them from different angles; they can use thinking tools to help them to choose and decide what they think is right. They are aware that they can tackle any problem using one device – their mind.

18

Tell me a story

All the fun's in how you say a thing.
Robert Frost 1874–1963

Children love to hear about real life happenings to real life kids! They also love to be told a story. Once you have read one of these little stories, tell it to your children in your own words. Make the story be about someone real – suggest that a friend of yours has another friend, whose son or daughter has made a fuss about this issue.

These stories should make car trips to school, waiting at swimming lessons or preparing a meal a time of chasing ideas. After a while you will be able to make up your own stories to illustrate or introduce Big Important Concepts that fit experiences your children are having. It's a bonus if you can sometimes (not all the time, or it can look planned) have a story to fit the situation or happening that is going on in your life at the moment.

These short stories are keys and should lead to fascinating discussions about Big Important Concepts.

The purple fuzzy jumper

There was this friend of a friend named Sam who'd fallen in love with a jumper. Not just any jumper but a cool, purple jumper! Two years ago, her cousin had been given this really great purple fuzzy jumper. It looked the softest warmest most fantastic jumper in the whole world. Talk about love at first sight. Sam saw it and just wanted it. As soon as she got in the car to go home, she said to her mum, 'Can I have one, oh please, Mum, please, please?' But of course she couldn't. Amanda's dad had bought it when he was in the United States on business and he couldn't remember the name of the store he had bought it at so she couldn't even write away to get one. For two years she watched Amanda like a hawk to see when she'd grow out of the jumper and yesterday was the day, the day, at long last, it was really hers.

This story contains issues of ownership, lending, borrowing, stealing, wants and must haves.

Some ideas to chase

* How will Sam feel when her grandmother says, 'You've got Amanda's jumper on'?
* Whose jumper is it?
* Why?
* Whose jumper would it be if, two years ago, Amanda said, 'I don't like purple – you have it Sam'?
* Whose jumper would it be if Amanda said, 'Here have a lend'?
* What is a lend?
* What if Sam stole it?
* What is stealing?
* Can stealing be right?
* If she steals the jumper and her mum gives it back, is Sam still a thief? What is a thief?
* Can you steal ideas?
* Is cheating stealing?
* What things can you steal?

The walking umbrella

This friend of a friend of mine has a nan who is getting a bit old and shaky. Nan is really vain and seems to think she is young, even though she is always falling over and hurting herself. The mum of my friend bought Nan a walking stick. But boy was she insulted; you think kids sulk! The mum then had an idea and got Nan a really glamorous, red satin, long-handled umbrella. Nan was thrilled to bits! That umbrella became her walking stick. So what? you say. Well, Nan relied on this umbrella so much she got a sore back from leaning on it and her back hurt. So they got her an artificial umbrella. A walking stick (nice and strong and long) with umbrella material stuck on it. And she's happy and now they're happy because her back's better, and she doesn't ring up my friend's friend groaning all the time!

This story concerns issues of reality, unreality and pretending.

Some ideas to chase

* What does 'real' mean?
* What does 'artificial' mean?
* Try to find things that look real and are real, things that are real but look artificial, things that are artificial and look artificial, things that look artificial and are real.
* Why do we call an artificial part of a body false?
* If you have a kidney transplant do you have a false kidney?

* Are false eyelashes false?
* What is a false front?
* Is a pacemaker a false heart?
* Do some buildings have false fronts?
* Can you put on a false front?
* Is smiling when you feel like crying false?
* Can words be false?
* Is being false wrong?
* What is a false friend?
* Is it false to wear glasses? When?
* Is a mask a false face? When?
* If you have stolen a passport is it a false passport? Why?

Who did that?

When you tell this story to your child you can tell it from a friend of a friend or as if it was an experience you had (wait till you've been to the doctor to tell it).

I was sitting in the doctor's waiting room the other day and a lady and her five-year-old son were sitting next to me when the son, suddenly and violently, vomited all over the waiting-room floor. I wished you had been there to see it! It was fascinating. The mother sighed and seemed to think it was the receptionist's job to clean up the steaming, very smelly mess, on the other hand the receptionist obviously thought it was the mother's job! They saw 'responsibility' and 'ownership' differently.

This story concerns issues of ownership and responsibility.

Some ideas to chase

* Was it the doctor or the surgery's responsibility to provide a clean environment?
* Should the receptionist clean it up?
* If the doctor owns the floor should he take responsibility for keeping it clean? (Should he have a bucket in a conspicuous place with a big notice saying CHUNDER HERE!)
* Was the mother responsible for the child and 'products' of the child?
* Is this different from the mother taking responsibility for graffiti done by an older child?

* Should the mother have come prepared with a bucket or plastic bag or asked for something 'just in case' when she arrived at the doctor's surgery?
* Should they both share the responsibility?
* Should the cleaner clean it up?
* Is the cleaner paid to clean up?
* Is the receptionist paid to clean up?
* Is there a difference between sick and dirt?

Hair today, gone tomorrow

The son of a friend of a friend made a terrible scene at the hairdresser's last Monday after school. When his hair was cut he crawled round the floor collecting his cut-off hair. His mother tried to stop him but he said, 'It's my hair and I can do what I like with it.' Then he told the story about some sultan he'd been reading about who kept every bit of his body that had ever been clipped off (nails and hair) in a bag he hung from his belt. Both the hairdresser and the boy's mum told him he was being disgusting.

This story concerns issues of ownership and belonging.

Some ideas to chase

* Who does the hair belong to?
* Is your hair always your hair?
* When is your hair not your hair? (If you sell it is it your hair still? If you dye it is it still your hair?)
* Is your hair part of you?
* Are your thoughts part of you? (Thoughts are words … can words belong to people?)
* Are your memories part of you?
* Are you part of your parents?
* Do your parents own you?
* Can people own people?
* What is a slave?
* Are your organs part of you?
* If you donate an organ and it is transplanted into someone else, whose organ is it?

And a pavlova

The daughter of a friend of mine felt that she was getting a little plump. She made up her mind to be careful of her diet and to stop eating any fattening foods. When she went to a party, the first thing she saw was a huge pavlova crammed with strawberries. When she went into the kitchen she saw a bowl of strawberries her friend's mother could not pack onto the pavlova. Phew, I'm safe, she thought. I'll just eat the strawberries. She ate the strawberries and yes, you've guessed it, she went on to eat a huge slice of pavlova. She couldn't help herself from helping herself.

This story concerns issues of temptation, choice, free will, and eating disorders and self-image.

Some ideas to chase

* What would you have done? Why?
* Was she free to choose?
* Did she choose what she wanted to?
* Are certain actions in certain circumstances inevitable?
* Can we predict what people will do?

Robin Hood

The son of a friend of a friend of mine was fascinated by the story of Robin Hood. He told his mum that he had all these questions going round in his head about Robin Hood. He said that Robin was the 'goodie' yet he was a thief. King John was the 'baddie' and yet he stopped people from shooting deer in the forest (which was good if you were a deer or you believed in letting wild animals live). King Richard was a 'goodie' yet he left his subjects to go and fight in the Holy Wars. How can war and killing be holy? None of this made sense!

This story concerns issues of priorities, being good and being bad.

Some ideas to chase

* Why did Robin Hood steal?
* Why did wicked King John stop people from shooting deer?
* Why did King Richard go to fight the Holy War?
* Can something bad happen out of a good intention?
* Can something good happen out of a bad intention?
* What are priorities?
* What different priorities do people have?
* Should we have priorities? (When discussing priorities you can discuss issues such as 'Should smoking be banned from restaurants?' Why? What should have a higher priority – enjoyment or health?)

Robin Hood: Goodie or Baddie?

When this friend of a friend was caught red-handed with someone else's skateboard, he was in a lot of trouble. He said that he was going to give it to someone who was very poor. He said Robin Hood was a thief and yet he was obviously a hero. Why wasn't he a hero too?

This story concerns issues of right and wrong, laws and stealing, reasons and excuses.

Some ideas to chase

* If you steal something that has been stolen already is that as bad as stealing for the first time?

* What is wrong with lying?
* Do you ever break rules? Why?
* What should happen to people when they accidentally break the rules?
* What should happen to people who deliberately break the rules?
* What is cheating?
* Do people believe that when a good rule is broken it is bad yet when a bad rule is broken it's good?

These stories are an amusing and entertaining way to open up important issues with your children. Your stories are a pleasurable way to let them see that there are many issues in simple things like having a haircut. Have fun making up your own stories. Your children will soon be pleading with you to 'Please tell me a story!'.

Hear yourself think

The really important stuff they never tell you ...
You have to imagine it on your own.
Brian Andreas 1956–

The aim of this book has been to encourage you to chase ideas and play around with your children; to think aloud about curious things, to solve puzzles and problems and to find your *own* way to discuss important issues, so that your children are empowered, curious, observant, positive, self-reliant and happy.

I hope you'll enjoy some wonderful thinking adventures with your children, and that these discussions will enrich your lives.

I anticipate that you'll find all sorts of interesting and important ideas to chase. Don't forget to discuss issues when your children have heard about an issue, or when you see something interesting on television or in the media. Start building your framework about 'truth', or 'fair' or 'real' by observing and talking when the idea is interesting to your children, but doesn't really matter. When the issue *does* matter, you'll be able to revisit and build on your earlier discussions.

Chasing ideas should enhance your children's awareness, confidence and thinking so that you all look at the world through new eyes. You'll find opportunities for wondering, for finding curious issues and puzzles to talk about, and for making up jokes to share with each other.

Perhaps you haven't read this book cover to cover, but if you've read about Enhanced Thinking and you have a handle on the Thinking Tools you're ready to *do it your way*. This book is for you to use and adapt, to find some examples of ideas to chase, with your children. Skim through the concepts and topics to find issues that are relevant and interesting to *your* children. I hope you have tried some of the keys to discussions, and built up your own discussions, then found your own keys and made wonderful discussions. I hope that your resources in your Thinking Trap Resource Book grow daily so you have a whole bundle of ideas to share and use and choose from.

There may be parts of the book you will need to revisit, to consolidate the ideas, or more importantly to see how you can adapt your *own* idea of a key to discuss some issues.

I hope that ideas contained between these pages can be like golden threads that will spread through the lives of your children: threads to bind and connect you together, threads to bind, connect and clarify ideas and understanding, threads to bind and support your children as they make informed, thoughtful decisions.

> We cannot do great things, only small things with great love.
> Mother Teresa
> 1910–1997

By taking the time, and making the effort to think about things with your children, you will have a great effect on their lives.

Enjoy chasing ideas with your children!

Chasing ideas in schools

Enhance the power of your students' minds to make them strong, able, clever thinkers.

Chasing ideas is a magic thing

My students love thinking aloud. As a teacher, I love chasing ideas with my students. Over the past ten years not a week has gone by without several students complaining that they don't have enough chasing ideas (Thinking Workshops). Recently, one student offered to pay me if she could attend more sessions! In handing the chasing ideas baton on to you, I'm passing on a wild and wonderful thing, an important, magical thing.

Chasing ideas is very much like quicksilver. Have you ever tried to pick up a droplet of mercury? One minute you have it, the next minute it escapes and breaks up into a cluster of droplets. The concepts we look at in *Chasing Ideas* are like that. They are intriguing, difficult, uncertain, and problematic. They are a mystery, and we can never entirely solve the mystery.

We can be detectives and look for reasons and clues and connections, we can unpack issues and look at them from other points of view, we can find and solve problems, we can try to find out why it is so, we can search for the 'absolute truth', but the nearer we get to 'the truth' the more complicated and elusive it becomes; the more we need to compare, classify, judge and reason. Hard, hard work! How often in a session I've heard, 'Help! My brain hurts from thinking … but let's do more!'.

Students become like bloodhounds: once they get 'the scent' of a new idea they whoosh off in another direction – frequently dragging a dazed teacher behind them! It's exhilarating, it's exhausting and it's also tremendous fun.

Here are some comments about thinking aloud from my students over the years:

* You can speak freely
* No-one is right or wrong
* You can share your ideas
* It makes you think harder
* I learn to express my thoughts
* It's fun listening to others
* It opens my mind
* It helps me look at things from a different angle
* When I am sad it helps me become happy
* I can let my feelings out
* It's good to express ourselves without being told we are wrong
* I love talking and thinking about things I usually don't notice
* It's freedom

In a recent discussion about the life of Marie Antoinette, ideas were being tossed this way and that. Ideas about responsibility, blame, ignorance, upbringing and rights were flying round the room until Steff grabbed the Thinking Ball of wool (see page 166) and exclaimed, 'I can't judge Marie Antoinette. I thought I could, and she was bad, but now I don't know. I do know I don't know her!' After discussing the Swiss canyoning tragedy, Jade, in Year 4, caught up to me after the class to explain that she could envisage and understand both points of view: that of taking risks for adventure and the view that life is precious so why should one take risks. Obviously these two ideas were flipping into and out of focus in her brain and she just had to share the exciting realisation that there were many points of view.

I am sure you can imagine the noise that emanates from my classroom. I have a firm belief that excitement and wonder and ownership of ideas and passion help to make the sessions of greater relevance and value to the students on a personal level. They are not just discussing ideas, they are connecting the ideas to their own lives and making sense of their thoughts.

Imagine you are at the cinema. The ads and 'trailers' are over then the curtains widen and the main film comes on, larger than life. This is a mental image I constantly try to hold in my mind – we are looking at life in great breadth and depth.

We can magnify small points until they fill the screen, so that we can examine each and every detail. When the camera pans back to the normal size, we understand one section of the whole. We are starting to make sense of the world.

Perhaps another analogy is to think of a globe of the world and travel. Even if you've read about certain countries and cities it is not until you have the experience of being there that you can feel you understand certain sections of the map. You know what it's like here, and here and here. That in turn helps you make links and connections to other areas. You can say to yourself, 'Such-and-such is like this … therefore so-and-so must be similar because … and dissimilar because …' You can start to make sense of symbols on the map and the world.

I believe each discussion we have with our students helps them to lay down layers of knowledge, a bit like those bottles of different-coloured sands in layers the students bring as a souvenir to show the class. These layers of understanding can be accessed and added to as connecting ideas come up in the future. It has been exciting to observe as students remember tackling an idea in the past, then add to and build on that idea. Just like opening a file on the computer entitled 'Truth' or 'Real', the computer of the mind accesses the files and ideas are opened up, changed, re-arranged and added to.

Perhaps I should explain a little of how I started on my thinking journey.

My journey

For over two decades I have been on a 'Quest', a search for the 'Holy Grail', the special heart of the curriculum. This quest has taken me from Mexico to Iceland, from New York to the deepest recesses of my own mind. I've been searching for that magic ingredient, which, when added to the 'beef and burgundy pie' that is the curriculum, will enhance and bring out the unique and special flavours of not only the beef but the mushrooms and the onions.

This special ingredient is not whipped cream to be placed beside the 'apple pie' of the curriculum but is rather an ingredient embedded in everything that is taught.

You can see how long this search has been, because the analogies are quite outdated – salt is a no-no and as for cream! Goodness, both are quite unacceptable!

My search for an analogy continued concurrently with my search for the ingredient, although the latter was becoming more and more obvious. One often searches with one's head in the clouds, as it were, when the answer lies at your feet! Then I stumbled on a stone and, holding the offending object in my hand, an old myth or story came into my head. The story of the 'Philosopher's Stone' – the mythical stone that could turn base metals into gold. If the Philosopher's Stone could turn metals into gold, I wanted a Philosopher's Stone that could turn discussions and chasing ideas into meaningful, precious experiences. Searching for the curious and the philosophical in a discussion with students can make the discussion profound and valuable.

Find your own 'Philosopher's Stone' stone and keep it on your desk where you plan your work, to remind you to look for the 'silver lining' of the curious in your class discussions. When you are planning your program, perhaps you could draw a symbol of a stone where you believe some curious ideas of interest could be embedded. As your students talk, listen carefully and don't be afraid to dig deeper by asking 'Why?' or 'How?' or 'Could you explain what you mean?'.

Thinking aloud could also be represented by the common cold. It's very contagious! Your students readily 'catch' it from you and each other! You can catch it from them. I can remember over a decade ago, teaching Year 4, when one day a student laughed and said, 'We've been chasing ideas all morning – from morning talk and news to reading and social education!'. They start to see connections; you see new connections and the whole school day can be thus enriched.

I can recall meeting a particular teacher at a conference. I was discussing what I do, and telling about some of the 'discoveries' or connections my kids had made when she took my hands and with great excitement and emotion said, 'I really need this! Tell me more!' After chatting for some time, this teacher and I had to go our separate ways, but we hugged as if we had been friends for years. She had caught the 'common cold' of thinking aloud. I do hope you will, too!

Chasing ideas: the I, eye, aye aye in education

I believe chasing ideas sessions are at the very heart and soul of education. Perhaps I could sum it up using the words of an old Mexican song, 'I, eye, aye aye':

I – to be able to know about myself.

EYE – to see issues with my mind's eye, to discover how and why I 'see' things in a certain way, to understand that other people may 'see' things differently.

AYE, AYE – to affirm, to make connections, to find links, relationships and patterns in life and help to make sense of the world.

In today's world I believe our students need time to ponder, to speculate, to explore and expand concepts, to look at issues of morality and ethics together, in a group, in a thinking commune. Students ask and question and develop skills in a congenial environment of tolerance, respect and cooperation. Perhaps when you are chasing ideas you could remind your students that you are all in a Thinking Aloud Co-op.

The classroom as a Thinking Aloud Co-op?

A Thinking Aloud Co-op fosters:

* a readiness to inquire, wonder, speculate, be critical, make hypotheses and infer
* awareness of thinking, comparing, deciding, judging, remembering, making connections, conceding, supposing and believing
* experience in communication, in speaking about one's ideas, in asserting, contesting, telling, proposing and stating propositions
* experience in listening to the ideas of others, an opportunity to practise reasoning, inferring, classifying, forming concepts, providing reasons, constructing definitions and justifying conclusions
* practice in observing, inquiring, measuring, describing, estimating, explaining, predicting and verifying; and reflection on one's own metacognitive process. This way the individual questions and examines not only the topic but the methods they are using to think about the topic. Thus they will be juggling the notion of what is a good question. They will ask, 'Is this reasonable justification for my point of view', as they are putting together their argument

* questioning and trying to understand common ideas that we use daily without thinking about them
* searching for meaning, meaning that is camouflaged in our ideas and statements
* wondering and 'digging deeper' into ideas
* 'flying higher' when thinking about ideas the reflective human mind finds naturally puzzling

> The individual student is empowered and all aspects of learning experiences are enhanced.

The outcome of a Thinking Aloud Co-op is clear: the development of positive self-concepts and self-esteem, development leading to responsible, thoughtful, creative, independent learners. Students are more curious, more aware and better equipped to cope with a future of change.

Why should I have Chasing Ideas Workshops?

A student's personal development can grow by chasing ideas. Chasing ideas in a Thinking Aloud Co-op prepares students to live effectively in the world by assisting them with their social communication and interaction skills.

A student's social development can grow by chasing ideas in a Thinking Aloud Co-op. Students appreciate, respect and analyse the views of others, resolve conflicts, negotiate solutions to problems, learn through listening to others, explain their concepts in a logical manner, maintain their own considered opinion and understand that values underpin judgements they make in everyday life.

Chasing ideas can activate the student's social awareness. By talking through issues in their Thinking Aloud Co-op, they can understand and appreciate more about the fundamental laws of morality that apply to acts of government, the legal system and the society in which they live. Students need to be more than well informed; they need a wide range of skills, their own value system, knowledge and understanding of what makes a democracy or a well-governed society, and habits of reflection and critical analysis.

Chasing ideas can help students make thoughtful, informed decisions. Many powerful issues (such as pollution, environmental concerns, armed, and ideological conflict and medical issues such as organ transplants) need to be considered very carefully with all points of view being considered.

Chasing ideas can provide an environment and opportunities for students to fossick around and find boundaries, limitations and possibilities. Thinking aloud concentrates on students' interests and enters into their quest to find out 'Why?' Thinking aloud builds on the wonder and puzzlement that is a characteristic of childhood.

Chasing ideas can influence the way students read and write. Children who are readers, write differently. Children who are writers read differently. Children who are thinkers read and write differently. For example, if folklore fairy tales and fables are studied by the children, themes of good versus evil, obeying one's parents, kindness repaid, curiosity, friendship, keeping faith, endurance magic and its power, obeying the law, totems and tribal magic, self-discovery, independence, responsibility and compassion could form the basis for many Chasing Ideas sessions. If an author is studied, the students could try to discover the ideas behind the books. Roald Dahl, for example, poses many curious questions in his books. Dahl stretches our imagination and forces us to look at reality and what is real: Can trees speak and communicate? Do giants exist? Do animals have feelings?

> Chasing ideas can be simply another focus in general class work or you can run Chasing Ideas Workshops or Thinking Aloud Co-op sessions.

How do I run Chasing Ideas Workshops?

Perhaps the most difficult aspect is that you, the teacher, must give up your power of intellectual autonomy. Everyone's opinion is valid and must be considered. When the children turn to you and expect a solution to a puzzle it can be difficult to say, 'I don't know. What do you think?' You have to be flexible enough to follow the conversation when it takes off in another direction from the one you expected.

During chasing ideas discussions you must be well prepared about ideas embedded in the topic, and you are the facilitator of the discussion – make sure that even the shy child has a chance to speak. Sometimes you might need to ask them a question.

At times you become the interpreter: 'Is ... what you mean?' when a child is experiencing difficulty expressing a point of view. It's up to you to make sure that all comments have a point – you'll find some children just want to tell a story. Find a 'nice' way to nudge them to get to the point.

Your Thinking Aloud Co-op group sits together in a circle (on chairs or on the floor with you as part of the circle, or a big Thinking Table – a bit like a boardroom table or dining table) so you're all able to see everyone and their reactions.

The classroom climate for your Thinking Aloud Co-op needs a mutually agreed Code of Behaviour: rules, expectations, rights and responsibilities.

'Thinking Ball' of wool

I find that using a Thinking Ball of wool is an excellent way to empower the students to run the discussions themselves. I start the 'ball rolling' by throwing the ball of wool to a student after I have introduced the topic we may (or might not) end up discussing. The students then throw the ball of wool to each other. Holding (and twiddling and playing with) the ball of wool works like a release; when the students have the wool it 'helps them think'. Twisting and unravelling the wool seems to free their minds. Also, at least once a session we simply pass the ball around the circle so everybody has a turn. (An interesting side benefit of using a ball of wool is that it is easier to say to a child, 'You've had the wool four times' rather than 'You're dominating the discussion.')

What should students do?

Listen to and respect others' ideas. Join in (everyone's view is equally important) and take turns, and refrain from dominating the discussion.

Ask for clarification or justification of others' opinions politely. Criticise ideas, not people. Probe others' opinions by asking in-depth questions. Be patient with others when they are explaining their concepts. Be patient when explaining concepts to others. Be careful not to interrupt people when they are speaking or they may lose their train of thought. Take care not to distract others.

Have fun! Good luck with this exciting expedition!

Think, think, think

Every day we are constantly making choices, evaluations and judgements; chasing, juggling and playing with ideas; comparing, guessing, 'reading between the lines'; continuingly, consistently, automatically thinking. But that doesn't mean we are always thinking well – we can all improve the way we think so that we think more effectively, logically and creatively.

There has been a worldwide focus on teaching thinking skills to promote learning and life skills. Unesco's Education For All has this as one of its goals. In the UK, since 1998, there has been the explicit inclusion of thinking skills in the National Curriculum. In the US, state and local curriculum guides contain goal and objective statements to support thinking programmes. Students need to be able to think well so they can live, work and function effectively in our current and changing society.

Today there is an added focus in education. To the study of the three Rs, 'reading, writing and arithmetic' (knowledge and information) has been added the three Is: initiative, ideas and innovation (thinking skills). It has been found that study of general school topics does not mean thinking skills are automatically enhanced. 'Thinking' is critical for students to organize and make sense of data collected in this information-led technological world. They also need to be able to communicate ideas and information, collaborate with others, and make rational, informed decisions.

Any Internet search using the words 'critical thinking' or 'thinking skills' will produce thousands of websites about 'thinking' – universities, teacher education facilities, centres for thinking, courses for developing critical thinking and advocates for thinking skills programs. The message is loud and clear: thinking skills can be promoted and will help students achieve their full potential, improving their study skills as they process ideas and arrive at reason-based judgements and become good citizens.

There is a demand from the work force for higher order thinking. More sophisticated thinking skills are needed in this 'information age' where thinking and inferring, problem solving multi-step problems, elaborating upon evaluations and interpretations of material, inventiveness, critical thinking, and questioning are paramount.

As parents we want our children to have successful and fulfilling lives. We want them to be happy, resilient and well-adjusted so they cope with life's ups and downs. We want them to think for themselves, form their own opinions, arrive at their own values and reach their potential. We can share the responsibility of the education of our children by assisting them to enhance their thinking ability and their decision making.

International 'thinking' conferences

There is an ever increasing number of teachers worldwide who believe that understanding more about thinking, and teaching their students about thinking is a priority. International 'thinking' conferences are held every two years with participants coming from over forty countries. Educationalists share discoveries and theories about the latest thinking about thinking, and inspire teachers to focus on the power and potential of their students' thinking.

Dr Edward de Bono

Any book about thinking is not complete without reference to and acknowledgment of the tremendous work by Dr Edward de Bono, who is author of over fifty books on thinking. In his book *Teach Your Child How to Think and Children Solve Problems*, de Bono says of thinking: 'Thinking is a skill that can be learned, practised and developed. The future of the world is going to require good thinking. Personal life has always required good thinking but in the future the increasing demands and opportunities will require even better thinking. In business and professional life, good thinking is essential for survival, for success and for competition.'

Edward de Bono's books assist people, including children, to think. He has played a major role in demonstrating good thinking can be learnt and practised. He works with education, business and governments, and is the originator of both the deliberate creative process of lateral thinking and the parallel thinking of the 'Six Hats' method. His CoRT program for teaching thinking directly in schools is widely used – and mandatory – in several countries.

Philosophy for Children (P4C)

Philosophy for Children has developed over the past two decades. It has spread worldwide from Iceland to Mexico, from Canada to Portugal. Philosophy for Children aims to sharpen the thinking skills of students through cooperative inquiry, so that the students think philosophically about ideas. From the detailed and thorough works written by Dr Matthew Lipman and Professor Ann Margaret Sharp, the movement has grown to include additional ways of examining philosophical issues.

The Philosophy for Children movement is built on the belief that children's puzzlement can lead them to think about many of the classic problems of knowledge, value and existence that have traditionally formed the core of philosophical thought.

Rich concepts in education

Most recent developments in the education of children under the age of twelve recognise that students' thinking is at the heart of education. 'Integrated Units' involve students' thinking. Teachers devise curricula based around a theme so students can study 'rich concepts' through which specific topics are developed.

There are also specific programs designed to challenge the thinking processes of students. These include Tournament of Minds and Future Problem Solving competitions.

Multiple intelligences

Professor Howard Gardner has looked at ways we understand or learn. In his book *Frames of the Multiple Intelligences* he suggests that everyone has different multiple intelligences. Gardner defines intelligence as 'the ability to solve a problem or fashion a product that is valued in at least one culture or community'. He stresses that no two people have the same combination of 'intelligences' and breaks the ways we think or function into the form of multiple intelligences. He has established that there are at least eight ways we understand and learn:

1. Linguistic (The child enjoys talking and playing with words, reads for pleasure and for information. They think in language or metaphors – for example a poet)
2. Logical mathematical (The child is curious, collects, counts, compares, categorises, plays with numbers. They enjoy taking a formula and applying it – for example a scientist)
3. Musical rhythmical intelligence (The child sings, hums and whistles in key a lot. They enjoy listening to or playing music and they love rhythm and rhyme – for example a musician)
4. Visual spatial (The child knows directions, likes drawing, remembers landmarks, manipulates visual ideas and makes pictures in their mind – for example an architect, a sculptor, or a surgeon)
5. Interpersonal (The child sees the idea from another person's perspective – for example a teacher)

> The different ways people understand and learn need to be taken seriously.

6. Intrapersonal (The child looks at how they are thinking and are aware of their own strengths and weaknesses)
7. Cognaturalists (The child has a keen interest in the world of nature)
8. Existential (The child is curious about who we are and the spiritual meaning of life)

Teaching in some schools may concentrate on the linguistic (using words), and the logical mathematical methods, as these intelligences are highly valued in Western society. Some students have other strengths or preferred learning styles – they learn and understand more by drawing, or working in groups and finding out what others think and know.

> As parents we can recognise the preferred way our children think and learn. We can encourage them to think and learn in this way, and also make them more aware of the usefulness of the other ways of learning.

Hemispheres of the brain

In considering a person's approach to thinking it can be interesting to know a little about the two hemispheres of the brain, and how each individual's dominant hemisphere can affect their thinking. Once we understand about the different functions of the two hemispheres of the brain, we can try to understand which hemisphere of our children's brains (and our own brain) appears to be dominant.

Frequently 'differences of opinions' arise because you and your child (or partner) 'see' things differently. For example I am a very right hemisphere dominant person; I always see the 'big picture', I work by intuition, and a picture is worth a thousand words to me. On the other hand, my engineer husband is very left hemisphere dominant. He can break the whole picture down to parts then concentrate on the parts; he's analytical, and verbal. With a very different view of the world it is often easy to judge that the other person is 'wrong' when they are just seeing things from a different perspective. I see the forest, he sees the individual trees and branches and leaves and roots. Together we make a good team.

Everyone's brain has these two sides – a left hemisphere and a right hemisphere. For best results in understanding, remembering and making sense of the world, both hemispheres work together as partners, each hemisphere complementing the other.

Both hemispheres receive messages. For most people, including children, one hemisphere becomes more efficient in dealing with the incoming stimuli. As this efficiency increases, that hemisphere assumes a dominant role. If the person uses perceptual strategies of the left hemisphere we say they are left hemisphere dominant. If they use perceptual strategies of the right hemisphere to organise their world, we say they are right hemisphere dominant.

Left hemisphere dominant

Left hemisphere dominant people are logical, critical, realistic and accurate. They focus on the facts, on how things work. They analyse ideas and pull ideas apart, they like to deal with words and figures. They like structured activities to learn, they deal with information sequentially, one thing after the other, they are organised and like things to be in their place, keeping to the rules, planning, being analytical, logical, factual and verbal.

Right hemisphere dominant

Right hemisphere dominant people are intuitive, imaginative, they see the big picture, they try to understand why, they like exploring and bending the rules, they learn by experimenting, they like to deal with images and pictures. They learn by discussing and sharing, they are spontaneous, they learn through involvement, they seem to sense what is right and they talk a lot.

* The left hemisphere analyses the known facts – the right hemisphere responds to the facts intuitively.
* The left hemisphere uses logic in handling information – the right hemisphere handles information spontaneously.
* The left hemisphere reduces the whole to parts, then reassembles the parts to the whole while the right hemisphere sees only the wholeness of information.
* The left hemisphere processes language into meaningful communication while the right hemisphere responds to tone, body language and touch.

* The left hemisphere is practical and is concerned with cause and effect while the right hemisphere is concerned with ideas and theories.
* The left hemisphere uses facts, the right hemisphere uses imagery.
* The left hemisphere is explicit and precise while the right hemisphere is symbolic, and representational.

For example the left hemisphere of the brain is active during study of reading, writing and mathematics. The right hemisphere of the brain is active when imagination, imagery, intuitive ideas are being thought about.

It is most important when thinking aloud with your children to provide opportunities for them to use both hemispheres of their brain: enrich imagery and intuitive thinking and focus on and expand skills in organising and analysing information in discussions.

Bloom's Taxonomy

Bloom's Taxonomy is a classification of thinking skills formulated by Benjamin Bloom, and this has been used by teachers for many years. The recognition of the importance of the taxonomy has waxed and waned, but it contains some interesting ideas about thinking. It is a useful framework to view the development of thinking skills and the different hierarchy of questions we can ask our children or our children can ask us. Even though Bloom considered young children incapable of higher order thinking, my experience does not support his view.

Knowledge

The base or foundation of thinking, this is memory and recall of information and is used to identify, recognise, examine and define the subject.

Comprehension

This is demonstrating that you have understood or comprehended the information. To do this you may need to explain, rephrase, interpret, describe and compare information.

Application

Applying the knowledge to a new situation or event.

Analysis

Using the information to identify cause and effect to examine the evidence including connecting, classifying, comparing, interpreting.

Synthesis

Using the information to make predictions or to help solve problems. Here you add to, design, imagine and hypothesise.

Evaluation

Information is used to judge, decide, evaluate and give opinions.

This very brief summary of just a little of the background theory behind *Chasing Ideas* indicates the interest and focus on thinking that is taking place throughout the world.

Albert Einstein believed that the purpose of education is to nurture thoughtfulness, to decide for oneself what is of genuine value in life – and then to find the courage to take your own thoughts seriously. By chasing ideas you will provide further opportunities for your students to do this.

Christopher Morley said that success is a journey, not a destination. Enjoy your thinking journey!

Author's notes

Page 7

'**Strong families bend in the wind ...**' – Associate Professor David Bennett, Head of Adolescent Medicine at The New Children's Hospital, Sydney; quoted in the *Sunday Age*, 9/7/2000

'**I knew I could do anything ...**' – Michelle Hamer, the *Age*, 8/6/99

'**Too little time,' says Barbara Holborrow** ... – Barbara Holborrow, *Kids*, Random House, Sydney, 1999

Page 12

In a study ... – This study was presented at the 7th International Thinking Conference, Singapore, 1997

... **greater wellbeing and calmness** – 'Dementia patients respond to pampering', the *Age*, 5/10/2000

Pages 48–50

These perceptually ambiguous images are derived from a figure by R. W. Leeper and E. G. Boring, two psychologists who, in 1930, adapted an anonymous German postcard (dated 1888). Leeper and Boring made the image famous in psychological circles; hence it is often referred to as the 'Boring figure'.

Acknowledgements

My father, who believed in me, and opened my eyes to the wonders and joys of chasing ideas. This has profoundly influenced my life, in an empowering and enriching way.

My students from Ivanhoe Girls' Grammar School, who have shared their thoughts with enthusiasm, humour and style.

The many colleagues with whom I have exchanged ideas over the last two decades and the inspiration gained from educational conferences and books. Edward de Bono, who has done so much to focus attention on the importance of thinking, lateral thinking and parallel thinking.

Jacinta di Mase and Jenny Darling for their early belief and faith in the book.

Bryony Cosgrove who chased ideas and came up with the title, and has once again guided me with grace and skill.

Chris Morgan for his wonderful whimsical cartoons.

Sean Doyle for helping pull all the pieces together.

Rex Finch who gave this manuscript the benefit of his expertise and knowledge.

Jane Smith for her help, Fabian Dattner and the Dattner family for 'rage of the heart', May Leckey for the ball of wool and the sun and moon exercise, and Ross Phillips for the broken vase scenario. Also Marie-France Daniel (Canada) and Zara Carniero de Moura (Portugal) for their encouragement and friendship.

Finally my heartfelt thanks for the interest and support of my family. To my husband Ted for his patience, support and help, to Rob for his insights and invaluable computer assistance, to Andrea for her input and encouragement, to Ken for his infinite patience and computer support, to Helen for her input of ideas and enthusiasm and to their partners Tony, Gabbi and Greg for their support and interest.

Sources

National Goals for Schooling in the Twenty-first Century: 10th Ministerial Council on Education, Employment, Training and Youth Affairs, April 1999, Adelaide, Australia

Quotes at beginning of chapters taken from Dr Peter Laurence, *5,000 Gems of Wit and Wisdom*, Treasure Press, London, 1977; Herbert V. Prochnow, Herbert V. Prochnow Jr, *A Treasury of Humorous Quotations*, Harper and Row, New York, 1969; Anne Stibbs, *Words of Women*, Bloomsbury, Market House Books, London, 1993

Brian Andreas, *Mostly True Collected Stories and Drawings*, StoryPeople, Indiana, 1993 (**www.storypeople.com**)

Benjamin Bloom et. al., *Taxonomy of Educational Objectives 1: Cognitive Domain*, McKay, New York, 1956

Clare Cherry, Douglas Godwin and Jessie Staples, *Is the Left Brain Always Right?* Hawker Brownlow Education, Melbourne, 1993

Edward de Bono, *Teach Your Child How to Think and Children Solve Problems*, Penguin, Melbourne, 1998

Michel Foucault, *The Order of Things: An Archaeology of the Human Sciences*, Tavistock, London, 1970

Howard Gardner, *Frames of the Multiple Intelligences*, Basic Books, New York, 1993

Barbara Holborrow, *Kids*, Random House, Sydney, 1999

Barry Humphries, *More Please*, Penguin, Melbourne, 1992

John McBeth, 7th International Thinking Conference, Singapore, 1977

Other books by Christine Durham

Doing Up Buttons, Penguin, Melbourne, 1997

Books contributed to by Christine Durham

There's So Much More to Life than Sex and Money, Sue Calwell and Daniel Johnson, Penguin, Melbourne, 1999

Coping For Capable Kids, Dr LeoNora M. Cohen and Dr Erica Frydenberg, Hawker Brownlow Education, Melbourne, 1993

Useful organizations

Art Costa Centre for Thinking

Arthur L. Costa writes about 'thought-full learning Communities' and the sixteen 'Habits of Mind'. These include: Persistence, Managing impulsivity, Listening with understanding and empathy, Thinking flexibly, Thinking about thinking, Striving for accuracy, Questioning and posing problems, Applying past knowledge to new situations, Thinking and communicating with clarity and precision, Gathering Data through all senses, Creating, imagining, innovating, Responding with wonderment and awe, Taking responsible risks, Finding humour, Thinking independently, Remaining open to continuous learning.

> 80 Marine Parade Road #09–05
> Parkway Parade Office Tower
> Singapore 449269
> Tel. 6353 4209; Fax. 6258 6234
> www.artcostacentre.com

In the US

Robert Sternberg PACE Centre

Robert Sternberg states that wisdom is especially important in current times. We need a balance between our own interests (intrapersonal), the interests of others (interpersonal) and the interests of the environment or our country (extrapersonal). Sternberg states that wisdom is not simply about information or what you know. It's about what you do with what you know – making a difference in real life decision and judgement making. We need to provide activities that draw upon wisdom, model wisdom and value wisdom. Sternberg foresees that in the end wisdom will prove far more important than knowledge and certainly far more important than raising IQs or test scores.

> Bob Sternberg
> Yale University PACE Center
> P.O. Box 208358
> New Haven, CT 06520-8358
> USA
> Tel. (+1) 203 432 4633; Fax. (+1) 203 432 8317
> www.yale.edu/rjsternberg

National Education Association (NEA)

The NEA provides information on how thinking skills instruction is fostered by US school curricula and offers helpful advice for parents on how they can improve their child's thinking skills.

> 1201 16th Street, NW
> Washington, DC 20036-3290
> USA
> Tel. (+1) 202 833 4000
> www.nea.org/parents/tools/thinking.html

Invent America!

This website's education program, for school or home use, helps children develop creative thinking and problem solving skills through invention.

www.inventamerica.com/kidskills.cfm

Leader to Leader Institute: The Child Art & Creativity Program

ICAF provides children with the opportunity to express their creativity and imagination through art, and to provide their teachers and parents a common platform to inspire children to visualize and shape their future.

320 Park Avenue, 3rd Floor
New York, NY 10022
USA
Tel. (+1) 212 224 1174; Fax. (+1) 212 224 2508
www.pfdf.org/innovation/innovation/innovation.asp?innov_id=185

In the UK

Sure Start

Sure Start is a UK Government programme that aims to achieve better outcomes for children, parents and communities.

www.surestart.gov.uk/resources/childcareworkers/inspiringcreativity/
Tel. (+44) 0870 000 2288
email. info.surestart@dfes.gsi.gov.uk

Curiosity & Imagination

Curiosity & Imagination promotes an approach to children's learning which harnesses the power of playful, hands-on experience as a tool for learning; empowers parents and carers to support their children's learning; encourages community ownership of the provision, giving children a central role in decision-making; and draws in expertise from local partners across a range of sectors.

Curiosity & Imagination 4Children
City Reach
5 Greenwich View Place
London E14 9NN
UK
Tel. (+44) 020 7522 6919; Fax. (+44) 020 7512 2010
www.curiosityandimagination.org.uk

Dialogueworks Thinking Skills

This website offers training in critical thinking and creative dialogue, both for professionals and for children.

www.dialogueworks.co.uk

Index